PRIVATE EYE ANNUAL 2011

EDITED BY IAN HISLOP

"Thanks, yeah, I'm good"

Published in Great Britain by
Private Eye Productions Ltd
6 Carlisle Street, London W1D 3BN
www.private-eye.co.uk

© 2011 Pressdram Ltd
ISBN 978-1-901784-55-8
Designed by Bridget Tisdall
Printed and bound in Great Britain by
Butler Tanner & Dennis, Frome, Somerset
2 4 6 8 10 9 7 5 3 1

PRIVATE EYE ANNUAL 2011

EDITED BY IAN HISLOP

*"More? There is no more! My generation
has used it all up, loser boy!"*

TWENTY THINGS YOU DIDN'T KNOW ABOUT WILLS AND KATE

Kate's middle name is Middlemarch, called after the racehorse Middlemarch which won the Derby in 1975.

Wills and Kate first met in Mrs McFothergill's Highland Fling Tearooms in St Andrews.

Will's first words to Kate were "Hi, ya, is this chair, like, you know, taken or anything?"

Wills and Kate share a passion for passion fruit, which they buy at Waitrose.

At the age of 11, Kate starred as Cinderella in the school panto. Contemporaries say she excelled in the role of the poor girl who gets the handsome prince. Uncanny or what?

Wills' pet name for Kate is "Widdecombe" or sometimes just "Widdy". This is apparently a reference to her shortcomings on the dancefloor.

Kate's nickname for him is "Your Royal Highness".

When she was a child, Kate had a pet tortoise called Queen Elizabeth II. It is still alive and is believed to be 100. Uncanny or what?

Kate's most watched DVD is "An Officer and A Gentleman", starring Richard Gere, which tells the story of a poor girl who wins the hand of a glamorous young naval officer. Uncanny or what?

The password on Wills' laptop is "Kate". Touching or what?

The password on Kate's laptop is "724XT3J".

Wills first told his grandmother, the Queen, that he wanted to marry Kate at the Braemar Games in 1985.

Four men had already proposed to Kate before she accepted Wills – Robbie Williams, Stephen Fry, Wayne Rooney and Oliver Letwin.

The Duke of Edinburgh has always had a soft spot for Kate and once took her seal clubbing in the Faroe Islands.

On a trip to Kenya, Prince Harry fooled the Royal couple by dressing up as Robert Mugabe and arresting them at gunpoint.

Kate has a secret tattoo on her ankle, showing the Hindu deity, Rushdi, riding on a dolphin.

Damien Hirst has been commissioned to create the first official portrait of the happy couple, showing them cut in two and swimming in a tank of formaldehyde.

When Wills told his grandmother that he was engaged to Kate, the Queen's response was to ask him "Have you come far?".

Prince Charles is keen for the couple to have a "fully organic wedding" and has offered to provide 1200 pots of Duchy Original fennel and raspberry yoghurt.

One of the first to congratulate the happy couple was the billionaire businessman Mohammed al Fayed, who sent them an email reading "Watch out for the fuggin' Duke of Edinburgh in his fuggin' white Fiat Uno".

For more things you didn't know (because we haven't thought them up yet), go to our Wedding of the Century website, www.wedding_of_the_century.co.uk

POPE FLIES IN

Boy, are my arms tired!

𝕹uremberg 𝕿imes
17 September 2010

COULSON ON TRIAL

The former head of Propaganda for the Nasty Party, Oberspinnerführer Andy Coulson, denied any knowledge of the thousands of victims of the infamous phone tapping which had taken place under his command. Several of his lieutenants have alleged that, as the senior commandant of Stalag Wapping, he was well aware of the crimes being committed by his underlings.

Coulson, however, claims no knowledge of the phone tapping. He said, "I had no idea that such things were being done in my name. And besides you have got nothing in writing. I was jolly careful about that."

Those Stigs In Full

The Eye's handy cut-out-and-throw-away guide to the Stigs they are all talking about

The Stig
Mystery racing driver who is in fact someone you have never heard of

Stig of the Dump
Mystery dump dweller who turns out to have fagged for Jeremy Clarkson at Repton (Is this right? Ed.)

Stieg Larsson
Mystery Swedish novelist who turns out to be dead

The Sti(n)g
Mystery lead singer of the Police who turns out to be rather boring (This is desperate. Ed.)

Stig Blomqvist
Not very mysterious Swedish rally driver who turned out to be 1984 World Champion in his Audi Quattro

Stiggy Legge-Bourke
Mystery Royal nanny who turned out to be called Tiggy and therefore not qualified for this (You're fired. Ed.)

Exclusive to all tabloids

YES! ROO ARE FORGIVEN

By Our Prostitution Staff **Lucy Morals**

LAST night Wayne Rooney answered his critics in the best way possible. He scored a goal, thereby putting behind him at a stroke all the tawdry revelations of the last week.

Forget the whoring, Wayne's back scoring! And that's all that matters.

The spud-faced nipper demonstrated with one masterful touch that it's all been a big fuss about nothing and it doesn't matter what he does off the field, so long as England are winning.

We say, *"Hats off to Wonder Wayne and stop complaining, Cry Baby Coleen – he's a national treasure and you should stand by him."*

And as for the critics who dismissed him as a useless has-been with a grubby personal life, well, shame on us for writing any old drivel that *(cont. p. 94)*

Spud-u-like   **Spud-u-don't-like**

K.J.Lamb

School news

St Crumpets

(Independent Fee Paying School for Girls, twinned with St Cakes)

Hooker term begins today. There are 385 girls in the school. Jeni Juici (Slappers) is Head Call Girl. Helen Wood (Escorts) is Captain of On-The-Games. Threesomes will take place on November 3rd, St Wayne's Day. The new Careers master will be Mr Max Clifford. There will be a performance of the school play, "The Best Little Whorehouse in Manchester" on Dec. 3rd. The School Tart prize will be awarded on Disappointed Parents Day, Nov. 24th, by visiting speaker and Old Crumpette, Belle de Jour (Harlots 1994-1997). The school orchestra will give a concert of Jeremiah Clarke's "Strumpet Voluntary" on December 15th. Tickets are available from the Bursar, Major Brothel-Smythe, c/o the Old Knocking Shop, Much Pimping, Beds. Sexeats are on Dec. 15th.

FOOTBALLER FAITHFUL TO WIFE SHOCK

*by Our Sports Staff **Juicy Jenni Murray***

AN emergency injunction last night was granted to a top Premier League footballer prohibiting us from revealing details of his private life.

The footballer, who cannot be named, is the subject of allegations that he is a happily married man who has not had sex either with prostitutes or with his friends' wives.

Lawyers acting for the footballer say he is "deeply hurt" by these "baseless smears" and will fiercely resist any attempts to ruin his reputation by publishing graphic pictures of him, his wife and their young son enjoying a day out at Alton Towers.

IS THIS THE END FOR LABOUR? YES

By Max Hastings

LIKE a pack of lemmings jumping over a cliff, the Labour Party has entered a mass suicide pact by electing an unknown extremist left winger to lead them into oblivion.

They have dug themselves a grave and now they are going to fall in.

KEEP GOING ED

By voting for an openly Marxist revolutionary Trotskyite who makes no secret of his desire to steal your house and give it to a family of asylum-seeking benefit scroungers, he has put a rope around the party's neck and pulled away the chair.

THIS IS VERY GOOD ED

No wonder the Tories are popping the champagne corks as they celebrate being in power for the next hundred years.

And all because Loony Lefty Labour have yet again shot themselves in the foot and turned the clock back to the bad old days of the 1970s by electing a leader even worse than Michael Foot.

Yes, welcome to Red Ed's vision of Britain, an all-too-familiar nightmare of streets full of uncollected rubbish, overflowing sewers, unburied corpses and giant rats roaming the land eating your toddlers.

But that will never happen. Because the British people are too sensible to fall for Labour's Stalinist agenda again. Which is why I can offer Labour's new leader only one sensible piece of advice: Vote Conservative!

ON OTHER PAGES

WHY we should not underestimate this very intelligent man ... 2
ED MILIBAND: Moderate statesman in the making? ... 3
WHY Miliband will win ... 94

 # BIBLICAL TIMES

Friday October 1, 10,000 BC   1 shekel

Cain wins in knife-edge finish

<small>BY ED SEA-SCROLL</small>

CAIN today emerged as victor in the fight to the death between himself and his brother Abel.

The surprise result left Old Testament prophets reeling after they had predicted that Abel would win.

The two brothers are the sons of Adam, a longtime labourer in the Garden of Eden, and Eve, an apple-eating vegetarian and snake keeper.

Miliband of Brothers

They were brought up together in a leafy suburban environment but it was always assumed that Abel, as his

name suggests, would be the favourite to be God's favourite.

Observers were therefore amazed when Cain challenged his brother in a leadership contest.

At the time Abel said, "Cain will only win over my dead body."

Now that Cain has triumphed, friends of Abel last night were saying, "Abel is gutted. He is too dead to speak."

None of them could answer the question as to what Abel would do next, but one insider said, "Probably very little because he is dead."

Cain, however, was unrepentant. When asked if he felt bad about bashing his brother's brains out with the jawbone of an ass, he quipped, "Am I my brother's leader? Yes, I am, as a matter of fact."

ON OTHER PAGES

● **Philistani Team accused of "throwing Goliath match".**

● **"I slept with David," claims Bathsheba.**

● **Scaremonger Noah accused of fabricating climate change data.**

THOSE REDS IN FULL

The Private Eye Guide to a Britain Lurching to the Left...

Red Ed Firebrand Labour extremist who is pledged to make Britain "a fairer society"

Red Ken Veteran Labour Firebrand who promises to extend the congestion charge zone

Red Riding Hood Firebrand Forest Dweller who is committed to protect the elderly against wolves

Red Wood Firebrand Conservative MP for Wokingham who is critical of the role of the Bank of England in the banking crisis

Red Bull Firebrand caffeine-based beverage committed to keeping you awake so you can get really drunk

(That's enough, Red)

THE ALTERNATIVE VOICE

VINCE SPART, Business Secretary. **Yes he's the Hard-Line Marxist Firebrand who is determined to Bring Down the entire Capitalist System. Now Read the Revolutionary Rhetoric that will lead to Anarchy in the Streets.**

Er basically... I'm not sure the banks have behaved frightfully well and er... really these bonuses are a bit much and er, I totally and utterly support British Business but surely er... thank you very much.

WHY WON'T ED GET MARRIED — Is He A Poof?

House prices plummet as Labour elect new leader.

Strictly Returns With Its Most Exciting Line-Up Yet!

They said that last year's Strictly Come Dancing contestants were B-list! Well, they are not saying that this year, as the BBC's top reality-celebrity-entertainment show unveils its incredible cast of Dancing Stars!

The Archbishop of Canterbury If he thought women bishops were tricky, wait till he tries the Tango!

Dame P.D. James Will she bring her impressive forensic intelligence to the all-important banter with Brucie?

Stephen Hawking Great at astro-physics, but can he pull off the comedy John Sergeant role?

Debo Duchess of Devonshire Her family back story is all very sad, but can she do the Cha cha cha?

Charles Moore Can the former editor of The Telegraph and biographer of Mrs Thatcher loosen up for the Latin American?

Mr Justice Eady Strictly's first legal contestant. But will this High Court Judge impress Judge Len Goodman?

PLUS Yet to be confirmed...
● Buzz Aldrin ● Nelson Mandela ● Sir Simon Rattle ● Professor Susan Greenfield
● William Rees-Mogg ● Her Majesty the Queen (You're fired)

GLENDA SLAGG
Fleet Street's XXX factor!!

■ HATS OFF to Ann Widdecombe, the one-time Tory Battleaxe who has become a National Treasure by a-dancin' and a-prancin' into all our hearts on TV's Strictly!??! Not for her a quiet retirement but instead wonderful Widdy has swapped the slippers and knitting needles for tap shoes and a spangly frock!!?! Who could fail to love her, as Waltzing Widdy trips the light fantastic with her handsome hunk of a partner, Anton du Berk!?!! Looking at you Ann, I just gotta get up and dance!! Dirty or otherwise!?!!

■ ANN WIDDECOMBE??!! Now I've seen all!! What a sorry sight to see this Frumpy Former Front-bencher a-stumblin' and a-bumblin', a-huffin' and a-puffin' like an old steam train round the Strictly dancefloor, making a complete fool of herself and giving poor old Anton du Berk a hernia!!?! Sexy Salsa??? Don't make me laugh!?!! Super Sad Act, more like (Geddit?!!?) Pack it in, Weighty Widdy and get back to the slippers and knitting needles!!?! Watching you, the last thing I wanted to do was get up and dance!!?! Dirty or otherwise (You've done this, Ed!!)

Byeee!!

From The Message Boards

Members of the online community respond to the major issues of the day...

Richard Dawkins condemns the burka

The sign at my brother's pub in Loughton says "No work clothes, no armed forces in uniform, no football colours, no Stone Island, no Burberry, no Boden, no burkas". And before you call him racist he's married to a coloured lady and she agrees with it. She's no oil painting but he wouldn't dream of making her hide her face in public – he'd rather we all suffered! Only kidding Pam, you look great (in the dark!)
– *Cyril_the_cabbie*

theres some well fit muslim bird's but theres some minger's out there whu need to wear a burka ☺ and a paper bag underneath in case it falls off! lol! – *Danny_Daz*

A muslim woman sat next to me on the tube today in order to surreptitiously read my newspaper. It's difficult to prove, because her veil shaded her eyes, but I distinctly heard her "tut" when I turned the page before she had finished an article on Afghanistan. I told her to buy her own copy, because if everyone read the Guardian without paying it would go out of business and there would be no national newspaper to represent enlightened opinion.
– *Emily*

Maybe have burka's for children so paedo's cant look at them?
– *Save_Our_Kids*

but small peados wud disguise thereselves in burkas and mingle with the kids – *Think_about_it*

Any short arse in a burka comes near my kids I swear Ill do time
– *Family_Man*

Let's all boycott muslim eggs.
– *Winnie*

And muslim bacon! – *Danny_Daz*

And muslim Murray Mints!
– *Murray_Maniac*

Great stuff guys! – *Bogbrush*

VAST CROWDS FLOCK TO HEAR SAINTLY FIGURE

by Our Religious Staff **Alexander Pope**

They said it would be a flop and that the tickets wouldn't sell. They said the faithful would stay at home.

How wrong they were!

When the tall, stooping figure of Sir Stephen Fry took the stage at the Albert Hall he was greeted by a tumultuous storm of polite applause from the massed ranks of his followers.

There was not an empty seat in the house.

Some people had queued all night to ensure that they would get a glimpse of the man who has been described as "infallible".

Fry, Fry and Fry Again

Said Kirsty Mole, 19, who had travelled all the way from Dumfries, "I've seen him on the telly, but nothing can prepare you for seeing him in person with his lovely smile."

There had been worries that Stephen's hardline dogmatic views on atheism, homosexuality and new technology would alienate the public, renowned for their tolerance.

But once he came before

them, raised his hand and uttered the traditional word "Bless", all misgivings were forgotten.

Even the most hardened sceptics were bowled over by his charisma and charming anecdotes about how he met Hugh Laurie at Cambridge.

By the end of his historic tour, there was no one in Britain who had not registered his essential message to the world – "Buy my new book".

FRY FILE

● **Fry is the leader of over 50 million "Twitterers", the fastest growing religion in the world today. He tells them what to read, what to think and what he's having for breakfast. Early in his life, Fry took a vow of celibacy, but not one of poverty. He is today estimated to be the 463rd richest man in the world.**

● All books published in Britain must be submitted to Fry for his stamp of approval. The book's cover can then carry the official imprimator "Gorgeous, fluffy and bed-wettingly amusing".

● **Fry is a world-renowned scholar, who has read over 10 million books and knows everything. His encyclical "Deus Mortuus Est" has been translated into two billion languages.**

● Insiders predict that Fry will soon canonise himself, not only for his astonishing intellect, but also for a number of miracles which have been credited to him. These include solving the Times crossword in a record 35 seconds, and appearing simultaneously in 27 different places (Dave, Dave Ja Vu, G.O.L.D, etc).

A Guide To Celebrity Vehicles

Pope Mobile

Dope Mobile

NEW POLL SHOWS PUBLIC BACK CUTS

by **David Nimbeeby**

THE PUBLIC today gave their strongest signal yet that they approved of the Government's plans to slash benefits paid to other people – as long as they kept receiving all the benefits they currently receive.

"Obviously benefits such as child benefit and tax credits paid to other people are unjustifiable and contribute to the feckless something for nothing culture," said 100% of taxpayers, "whereas the benefits I receive such as child benefit and tax credits are used responsibly to help create the Big Society that David Cameron aspires to."

"So as long as everyone else gets their money slashed and I don't, I'm fully in favour of the Government's proposals."

Child Benefit – Winners & Losers

Losers

Couple with three children, father earning more than £43,875 and mother staying at home will lose £1,752

Winners

Couple with three children, millionaire father earning £142,500 and millionairess mother staying at home will lose £1,752

WELL, thanks a bundle Mr Osborne from all of us hardworking middle-class mums!!

Cutting child benefit is a slap in the face to the very people you should be trying to help!

If you just stop playing with your calculator for a minute and look at the threads on Yumsnet*, you'll see just how angry we all are. In a single stroke you've removed the one little bit of slack that we allow ourselves in the endless grind of juggling work, childcare and maintaining the fragile egos of our useless partners (yes, you, Simon, stop watching Claudia Winkleman on your iplayer – she's way out of your league).

This is nothing less than an attack on women who look after children – as I explained to our Cambodian au-pair Hah Dhup, when I cut her allowance in half. Suddenly all those little luxuries that child benefit allowed, like lunch, are now a thing of the past

POLLY FILLER

for poor Hah Dhup. Now she will just have to knuckle down 24/7 to the half-term grind of taking toddler Charlie to see *Despicable Me* for the tenth time (in 2D by the way – I'm not paying extra for some stupid 3D glasses) and picking up my Stella McCartney handbag from Downton's Drycleaners after it got splashed with fizz at the Style Awards! (Thanks, Celia!)

SO, Mr Osborne, next time you want to attack the women of Middle Britain or *Mimmen* as I call us in my hilarious yet angry new collection of columns, *Au What a lovely Pair!* (Johnson & Pearson, £19.99), just think who you are really hurting – poor unfortunate women like me who have to put up with the silly girl Hah Dhup crying all the time!

* The social networking site for serious career women who are committed mothers and just happen to be quite yummy.

A PASSAGE TO INDIA

by Dame Sylvie Krin, author of *Heir of Sorrows, Duchess of Hearts & You're Never Too Old*

THE STORY SO FAR: Charles has been invited to Delhi to open the Commonwealth Games. Now read on...

THE Indian sun blazed down from a cloudless sky as Charles's stretch rickshaw swept down Viceroy Street, now renamed Manmohan Singh Avenue, scattering the sacred cows and the scores of street beggars queueing up outside the Star Of Bucks Coffee House.

Charles, with Camilla by his side, was delighted by the colourful scene. How amazingly India had changed since the days when Diana had posed for that sulky photograph in front of the Taj Mahal.

The new India was alive and brimming with hope for the future, as indeed was Charles himself.

Here he was about to step to the centre of the world stage to open these games in place of his mother.

Billions of eyes would be on him as he delivered what would be the most important speech he had ever made.

As his rickshaw skilfully navigated its way past the flooded potholes, and ragged street salesmen offering him free broadband connections for only 300 rupees as month – "Very good, very fast, Sahib" – Charles read through the draft of the speech on which he had been labouring for months.

There were the headings of his great message to the world – "Climate Change – greatest challenge to mankind – it really is appalling – global warming – even more appalling – environmental catastrophe – need for wind farms and organic yoghurt –

not appalling at all – mater sends best wishes."

Within only an hour or two now his big moment would at last have arrived...

"WHERE is everybody?" asked Charles, as he and Camilla walked into the vast Shilpa Shetty Stadium, gazing down on the rows and rows of empty seats below him.

"Test match today, Sahib," explained a deferential Indian official. "Very important game, Australia v. India. We all have a lot of money on what's going to happen in the third over after lunch."

But Charles scarcely heard this. "So when am I on?" he asked expectantly.

"It's quite a short speech, and shouldn't take more than three hours".

The turbaned functionary smiled enigmatically, as he gestured for Charles and his consort to sit in their place of honour on the official dias, which a number of workmen were still hastily constructing.

As they sat down, on two wobbly chairs, a great throng of Indian dignitaries arrived to take their seats around them, and the colourful opening ceremony began. Charles could hardly wait...

"HOW long will I have to wait?" he whispered to Camilla, as one dignitary after another made longer and longer speeches in a bewildering array of local languages.

Finally it was his turn. Charles strode to the rostrum, pulling his own speech from his pocket, ready to deliver his golden words to a waiting world.

But as he reached the podium, the turbaned official intervened. "This is what you have to say, Sahib," he whispered.

Charles looked down at the scrap of paper he had been handed and read it in disbelief. Was this all he was allowed to say – after he had spent all those months labouring in his beloved study in Highgrove?

"Pleased to hurry up Sahib," murmured the official, "we are running late."

Charles looked out mournfully at the thousands of empty seats below him and read out the message on the paper he had been given.

"My mother declares that the Games are now open. Good luck to you all."

He had barely finished when there was an ominous crack and the podium gave way, sending all the dignitaries crashing to the floor in a cloud of paper, flowers and dust.

"This really is appalling," thought Charles, as he picked himself through the rubble. How could it get any worse?

"So sorry, Sahib," said the official. "It is indeed appalling – and I can only offer our very deepest apologies to you and your beautiful wife, Diana."

In the distance a sacred cow mooed loudly and there was an ominous rumble of thunder as the monsoon returned.

UNEMPLOYMENT SHOCK

It's the Big Issue Society!!

*"Pleased to meet you, gosh, I hadn't realised there was a **Lord** Gaga"*

Tonight's TV recipe
Pizza

Ingredients

1 Telephone
1 Credit card

Instructions

Phone up local pizza shop and await delivery.

Comments

Takes 20 minutes.
Serves 4.

KNACKER SLAMS PUBLIC OVER 'CHELSEA BARRISTER TRIUMPH'

by Our Police Staff **Sir Robert Marksman**

LORD KNACKER of Yard, formerly Chief Inspector Knacker of the Yard, hit out today at public criticism of police tactics in the recent Markham Square siege.

Said Lord Knacker, "The public have no idea of the complexity of the situation in which we found ourselves. They are totally ignorant of police procedures and make inaccurate assumptions based entirely on watching BBC news".

The Old Kill

Asked why it was necessary to deploy 59 armed officers and a helicopter to deal with one man with a shotgun, Lord Blair replied, "Our job is to protect the public and we were confronted with a man who could easily have been armed with a nuclear weapon and was unafraid to use it."

He continued, "Our aerial reconnaisance showed that Chelsea is full of houses, many of

them with people in them and all of them could have become victims of this madman with an atom bomb."

He concluded, "Naturally we regret the outcome of this sad incident as, in my judgement, the young barrister, as we now know the victim to have been, would have made an ideal member of the police force – firing randomly at passing civilians."

Shooting mouth off

Other senior officers were quick to support Lord Knacker. Chief Inspector Knackerson told reporters, "It is time for members of the public to stop attacking the police for simply doing their job. I must warn them all that if they continue to do so they run the risk of being shot."

Adult chat lines

PAEDOPHILE SEX TOURIST WAS ARTIST – SCAM

by Our Gallery Staff **Jacques Tahiti-Modern** and **Polly Nesia**

IN A sensational new exhibition of the renowned pervert Paul Gauguin, curators are trying to claim that the notorious sex fiend was secretly a talented painter with a gift for vibrant colours and *(cont. p. 94)*

That Honorary Degree Citation In Full

SALUTAMUS DONALDUS TRUMPUS MERCATOR ET MULTIBILLIONAIRUS TYCOONUS AMERICANIS SPECULATOR ET INVESTOR IN HOTELI ET CASINI ET ESTATUS REALIS IMPRIMIS 'TRUMPUS TURRI' IN NOVUS YORKUS MONUMENTUM ENORMIS ET SYMBOLICUS PHALLICIS DE SYSTEMUS CAPITALISMIS CELEBRISSIMI IN AMERICA PER CAPILLI RIDICULI TRANSPLANTUM PROBABILUM ET PER PROGRAMMUS TELEVISUALIS 'DISCIPULUS' IN QUOD DICAT CATCHPHRASUS 'TU EST IGNIS' (ALANUS SUGARIS ALBIONIS EQUIVALENS SED MULTUM PAUPERIORIS QUAM TRUMPUS) DIVORCUM ACRIMONIS DE FEMINA IVANA TRUMPA UNPOPULARISSIMUS IN CALEDONIA PROPTER VULT CONSTRUERE CURSUM GOLFUM MASSIVUM IN ABERDEENSHIRE ET CONSEQUENTE POPULI CALEDONI TRUMPUS ODIUNT IAM INCREDIBABILE DICAT UT VULT CURRERE PER PRESIDENTE STATI UNITI ANNO DOMINI MMXII GAUDEAMUS IGITUR!

© Robert Gordon University, MMX.

Who Are They – Ed Miliband's New Generation?

In the biggest shake-up in the Labour Party's 100-year history, new leader Ed Miliband today unveiled his shadow cabinet, which he described as "a totally fresh, new and exciting team to take Britain into the 22nd Century".

Out Goes Discredited former Deputy Leader **Harriet Harman**, 69, whose many gaffes paved the way for Gordon Brown's defeat.

In Comes **Harriet Harman**, 35, highly respected former Deputy Leader whose good sense and judgement will ensure Labour's victory at the next election.

Out Goes Elderly, bland, former postman **Alan Johnson**, 78, who once admitted, "I am not up to the top job".

In Comes **Alan Johnson**, 42, visionary high-flyer, whose knowledge of the postal system will guarantee Labour victory at the next election.

Out Goes Husband and wife team **Ed Balls**, 53, and **Yvette Cooper**, 47, both tarnished by their close links to Gordon Brown.

In Comes Wife and husband team, **Yvette Cooper** 21, and **Ed Balls**, 28, both distinguished economists with wide experience of bringing the country to its knees. *(Is this right?)*

Out Goes **Ed Miliband**, 42, dim policy wonk and author of the manifesto that lost Labour the last election.

In Comes Labour's saviour, **Ed Miliband**, 19, whose knowledge of policy is unrivalled and who is sure to create a new manifesto that will spur Labour to a landslide defeat. *(That's enough New Generation. Ed.)*

Out Goes **Andy Burnham**, **Caroline Flint** *(I said that's enough. Ed.)*

If you would like to know more about the boring changes to the Shadow Cabinet, visit our website www.zzz.org and have your say, which we can then put in the newspaper tomorrow in our "What The Bloggers Say" column, which replaces the old News section which we had to pay people to write.

NEW BORIS SHOCK

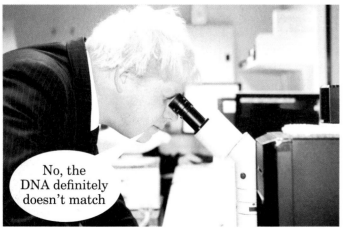

No, the DNA definitely doesn't match

HYPNOTISM It works!

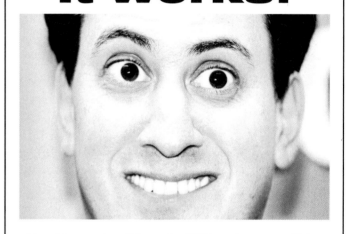

Top Mesmerist, **Edwardo Milibando**, says, "All you have to do is look into my eyes and you will fall into a deep sleep. When you wake up you will have forgotten everything that has happened in the last 12 years, and when I snap my fingers you will vote Labour no matter what people tell you."

To experience this life changing experience for yourself contact Milibando, the Great Delusionist, c/o Kinnockio Cabaret and Music Hall Entertainments, Flat 39b, Leytonstone High St. (Knock loudly and ask for Neil).

NEW OLD SAYINGS

Give a man a fish, he'll eat for a day.

Teach a man to fish, he'll greedily over-exploit the fish stocks, create unsustainable seafood levels, and starve.

THOSE ARMED FORCES

How They Will Look

AFTER the most savage cost-cutting blitz for centuries, Britain's defence forces will be reduced to their lowest level since the Norman Conquest.

Here is a cut-out-and-keep guide to what you will see.

ROYAL NAVY

To be reduced to three pedaloes based at Hastings, ready to repel any conventional armed intervention above Threat Level 3. HMS Flintoff, HMS Teletubby and HMS Trouser Press will not be equipped to carry fixed-wing fighter support aircraft until 2046 and will be moth-balled for three years on completion and then sold to the Taliban Navy.

ROYAL AIR FORCE

To be reduced to one hot-air balloon kindly lent by Sir Richard Branson bearing the logo "Get it up with Virgin".

This unmanned drone balloon will perform a dual role, by providing surveillance of any invading forces (Level 7, Green Alert) and to provide a ceremonial fly-past over Buckingham Palace on important national occasions (eg. final of Strictly Come Dancing).

BRITISH ARMY

To be reduced to a single battalion of highly-trained computer operators to fight against cyber attacks by terrorists and other foreign powers.

The new King's Own 17/21st Googlers will be based in Bangalore.

TOP GENERAL HITS OUT AT DEFENCE REVIEW

By Thomas the Tank

THE Grand Old Duke of York today warned that proposed troop cuts by the Government would seriously compromise his ability to march up and down hills.

"I need ten thousand men," he said, "to effect a successful marching up the hill strategy and without ten thousand men it would be impossible to implement a marching down the hill strategy."

Leaked plans to reduce the Grand Old Duke's force to just ten men have been defended by Nurseryland's Ministry of Defence. Said a spokesman, "In today's economic climate the Grand

Old Duke of York cannot get away with special pleading on behalf of his ten thousand men."

He continued, "The Navy will be down to one ship – a pea green boat – and the Royal Air Force will consist of a single sparrow armed with a bow and arrow. The Duke of York will be very lucky to have ten men."

"Ok, chaps, we rendezvous here 0900 hours"

HOPE FOR MILLIONS

Unemployed man found a job in the community

by Our Employment Staff **Gazza Job**

A MAN who was once told that he was "useless and unemployable" has been given a new sense of purpose thanks to David Cameron's new initiative to "get the jobless back to work".

Iain Duncan Smith, 63, used to run the Conservative Party but was made redundant when colleagues decided that he was "too quiet for the job". He also had an embarrassing cough which he claimed was the real reason he was given the sack.

For some years Iain Duncan Smith found it hard to get any work.

"I was at a low ebb" he confessed, "I did apply for a job as a supervisor in a cough sweet factory but they said I was too quiet".

But then Duncan Smith's luck changed overnight when the Prime Minister plucked him from obscurity and put him in the Cabinet. Cameron said, "As a former member of the long-term unemployed and useless, Iain is exactly the person to run the benefit and welfare system".

Said Duncan Smith, "Er… Hum…" when asked to speak up he said "ER…HUM!".

MODERN NELSON

I see no ships

That's the spending review for you

DIARY

RACHEL JOHNSON

July 19th 2009

I've just been appointed editor of The Lady magazine! Not bad for someone who's never read it – and never will!

July 20th

I go to the newsagent's and ask for a copy of The Lady magazine – just to see what I've let myself in for!

To my horror, the newsagent expects me to pay for it! Crikey! He must think I'm a terrible old fuddy-duddy!

July 21st

Wake up! My first day as editor! I suppose that means I'll have to go into the office – groan!

Arrive early just before lunch and agree to take a peek at the mag. Long dreary articles on gardening and stately homes and tweed skirts. Wot, no sex? Bor-ring! Groan!

July 22nd

Introduce myself to staff! You'll never guess who I am, I say – I'm Boris's sister!

July 23rd

Sick to death of hearing staff telling people I'm Boris's sister. Hey guys, I say – why go on and on about it? Is it just because I'm Boris's sister?

July 24th

My new mission: to halve the age of the reader. Average age of reader: 80. Ting! Brill brainwave! Phone downstairs and tell boxwallahs to cancel the subscription of any reader over 40!

July 25th

I've managed to halve circulation overnight! But daft prat owner Ben looks distraught! "Durrh!" I tell him. "That's what you wanted, dick-face!" But he still looks upset. Memo to self: toffee-nosed fatso Ben can't take a joke! Best be more tactful in future!

July 26th

Staff all walking around with hangdog expressions on their elderly grey faces! Gather them for a cheery pep talk! Explain in words of one syllable that the mag's bloody boring and most of them can expect the Order of the Boot any time now – but, hey guys, let's keep our sense of humour, shall we?!!! No one likes a miseriguts!

July 27th

Must get round to sacking some of them! TV cameras are coming tomorrow so best to wait until then!

July 28th

The TV cameras are here to record my every move! Wear a plunging neckline, and adopt my trademark "Hello, boys!" pout as I perch on my desk with a nice bit of leg showing! The TV people ask me to leaf through a copy of the magazine. What magazine? I say. The Lady, they reply. Come off it, boys, I say, who do you think I am? I'd normally read something much more interesting than that!

July 29th

With the cameras rolling, I have a one-on-one with Julie something-or-other, the assistant editor. But after two minutes, it turns into a one-on-none – I've just given her the sack!

But then the TV director says the lighting was all wrong, and could we do it again please! So I call Julie Thingy back and sack her again, this time crossing and uncrossing my legs!

Non-swanks, but this time the director says it's perfect!

July 30th

I tell the cameras to roll before calling in the literary editor and giving him the boot!

I'm really getting the hang of this telly stardom business!

Lunch with super-hot Katie Price, aka Jordan. The lady's got class – and our regular bridge column really needs hotting up.

July 31st

So much to do, but I still manage to make it to the office by the afternoon, ready for a bit of me-time. But no sooner have I got here than my new assistant editor drops a major bombshell: we've got no articles for the next issue!

Emergency stations! Don thinking cap! Ting! Brainwave! Hey, guys – let's use the old articles from the last issue! No one will have read them! Brill!

August 1st

Watch my son play rugby and have lovely time standing around in Wellies commissioning other bored Dragon School yummy mummies to knock off articles for The Lady! I give them each a pen and paper and by the end of the game we've got a fresh stock of twelve fabby new articles!

August 2nd

Call Deborah, the super-glam Dowager Duchess of Devonshire, no less (!) and invite myself to Chatsworth. Her butler tells me she's not available! Typical Debo! Talk about a sense of humour!

I decide to give her the most almighty surprise by driving straight to Chatters and barging in!

"Cooeee, Debs!" I say. No reply! I search all over the place, and eventually find her cowering behind a sofa!

Playing hide and seek – and at her age! "You Incorrigible Mitfords!!" I laugh. "Come on, you old bat!" I say, setting her at her ease before getting down to business. "Give us an article!" That's what they call pulling out all the stops! Talk about a charm offensive!

August 3rd

Oodles of letters from elderly (bor-ring!) readers cancelling their subscriptions. I've got rid of all those dreary articles on lumbago and budgerigars and azaleas and put in totally hot new pieces on how to make your man sizzle in bed, who's who on the X Factor, what Sadie told Sienna and the greatest shags in Notting Hell – and they're still not satisfied! They just don't get it, do they?

As told to CRAIG BROWN

"Aren't they cute when they talk like little adults?"

WEDDING OF THE CENTURY

How They Are Related

Russell Brand

Bertram Russell
|
Lord Russell of Liverpool
|
Lord Russell of Spring
|
Marlon Brand
|
Jo Brand
|
Russell Twisk
|
Jane Russell
|
Russell Harty

Katy Perry

Fred Perry
|
Perry Worsthorne
|
Perry Mason
|
Grayson Perry
|
Katie Middleton
|
Perry A. Water
|
Katie Price
|
Suzi Perry

(The nuptials were conducted by His Holiness Sir Harry Krishna)

Nursery Times

Friday, October 29, 2010

TEA PARTY CANDIDATES ROMP HOME IN WONDERLAND MID TERMS

by Our Election Staff **Lewis Carol Thatcher**

A GROUP of eccentric Tea Party attendees, including the Mad Hatter, a White Rabbit, a Dormouse and a girl called Alice, are set to pull off an incredible victory in Wonderland.

Despite clear evidence that all the candidates are clinically insane, voters across Wonderland are flocking to them in their thousands. These are just some of the Tea Party's radical credos:

● The Mad Hatter believes that President Obama is a Muslim sent by Satan to encourage masturbation.

● The White Rabbit refuses to allow any coloured rabbits into his burrow.

● The Dormouse is

permanently asleep.

● Alice is a hot-diggety born-again Hockey mum whose children have yet to be born but who believes in having the occasional drink from the bottle so that she can either "walk tall" or "support a smaller state" *(That's enough Tea Party, Ed.)*

On Other Pages *Landmark Pre-Nup case. Owl to keep money, honey and pea-green boat. Pussycat to appeal.*

Those Kennedys In Full

Not Drunk

Not Drunk

Not Drunk

"I'd really hoped they'd leave home after Uni"

SARAH PALIN TO RUN FOR PRESIDENT IN 2012

Armenia needs me

THE AMERICAN PEOPLE
An Apology

IN RECENT years, in our coverage of American politics, we may have given the impression that, in electing Barack Obama as President in 2008, the American people had shown themselves as thoroughly enlightened and forward-looking, having thrown off racial prejudice and generally become politically mature in a way which should serve as an inspiration to the whole of mankind.

Such headlines as "US Comes of Age in Electing First Black President", "Obama Victory Shows America Has Thrown Off Race Prejudice For Ever" and "US Walks Tall Into Future With Barack The Superman" might have suggested that we considered that by electing Mr Obama, America was entering a new golden age.

Having watched with horror as in the recent mid-term elections US voters went overboard for candidates representing the so-called Tea Party, we now realise that the American people are no more than a bunch of backward-looking, reactionary, gun-toting, Bible-bashing rednecks who have no place in the modern world. We apologise to our readers for any inconvenience our gullibility may have caused.

'A Gross Miscarriage of Justice'

by Lord Gnome

I WISH to protest in the strongest possible terms at the grotesque fine of £25 imposed on me by the House of Lords Standards and Privileges Committee, following an absurd misunderstanding over my parliamentary expenses.

The Committee has seen fit to misinterpret my explanation as to why I very properly made a claim for £2 million in respect of my living arrangements.

As I had made clear to the Committee, I quite correctly registered as my second home my humble country mansion *Gnome Towers*, on which it was necessary for me to claim a number of essential refurbishments, such as the replacing of gold taps, the reconditioning of a heated swimming pool (including a solarium and sauna for the use of my diary secretary Ms Rita Chevrolet) and the essential pruning of a giant *wisteria cameronia* which was threatening to obscure the light in the library where I study important parliamentary papers (the *Daily Telegraph*).

My primary residence for the purpose of my parliamentary duties is of course a caravan parked in a layby on the M40.

Although I have not visited my primary home for some years, it provides much-needed accommodation for a family of Romanian sex workers, whom I have, as a philanthropic gesture, taken under my wing.

I have never made any attempt to conceal any of these facts, which makes it all the more disgraceful that the Committee saw fit to impose on me a penalty so draconian that I have been obliged to claim it as a legitimate expense.

15

Extracts from the most important book ever to be written by a retired vicar,

A JOURNEY OF FAITH

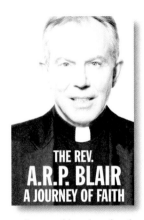

THE REV.
A.R.P. BLAIR
A JOURNEY OF FAITH

CHAPTER ONE
The Road Begins

WHEN I was a little boy I was already aware that I was destined for great things. Don't get me wrong. I didn't have any Messiah Complex or anything!

But, hey, I was a public service kind of guy from day one. I've always wanted to help other people from before I was born.

My parents tell me that I helped an old lady across a very busy road when I was still a toddler and could scarcely walk myself.

People can criticise me for that if they like. But in the real world, hey, you have to do the right thing.

CHAPTER TWO
The Calling

IT was not only the Rev. Martin Luther King who had a dream. I had one too. But mine was kinda different!

It happened in 1994 when I had this dream that our vicar, the very well-respected John Smith, had suddenly died of a heart attack and gone to heaven.

And you know what my very first thought was? In my dream I heard myself say, "Great, I must have his job". And I heard this voice, like an angel or something, saying from above, "Go for it, Tone, you are the chosen one!".

When I woke up, Cherie was holding me in her arms. "What's wrong, Tony?" she said.

And you know what? I didn't say a thing. It wasn't a time for talking. It was a time for raw animal passion. I needed her strength. I needed the comfort of her willing body.

With one bound, I tore the flimsy negligée from her heaving... hey, guys, I don't want to go into too much detail here.

Some things are, you know, private. Suffice to say that everything in my dream came true. And that's how I got the best job in the world, to be the Vicar of St Albion's.

Was that divine intervention? It's not for me to say. But in my personal opinion it was!

CHAPTER THREE
The Triumphal Entry Into The Vicarage

I SHALL never forget the day of my arrival in my new parish. As I approached the door of the vicarage, a huge crowd of ordinary parishioners greeted me, waving little union jacks kindly handed out to them by Mr Campbell, a great guy but, sadly, a bit mental!

What a day it was!

And then guess what one of my very first jobs was? Hearing confession from Princess Diana, no less!

I know vicars shouldn't reveal these sort of confidences, but as she has, sadly, passed away and gone to heaven, I know that she wouldn't mind! Let's say for a start that she was absolutely stunning and had great legs!

I know vicars aren't meant to notice these things – especially when they're married to someone as lovely as Cherie – but she had the kind of smile that said "How about it, Rev?".

Anyway, I warned her that she should beware of her new boyfriend, Dodi Fayed, and that under no circumstances should she go to Paris and get in a car with a drunken driver and not put on a seat belt. I mean, talk about dreams coming true! Here was another one.

But, sadly, she didn't listen to me because, frankly, she wasn't there and I may have imagined the whole thing.

But that doesn't mean it wasn't true! And the really important thing is that at her funeral I preached a sermon which has been described by many people as "the most moving sermon ever preached by anyone".

Mr Campbell says he helped me to think up the phrase "the People's Princess", but, nice guy as he is, he is a bit prone to taking credit for other people's achievements (a bit like everyone else I've ever worked with!).

CHAPTER FOUR
The Church Militant

NOW comes the sticky bit! I know that! And I know that many of you think I made a terrible mistake in supporting the Rev. Dubya, leader of the Church of the Latter-Day Morons over the whole Iraq business.

I respect your opinions but, frankly, you're wrong! We can go over all the evidence till kingdom come, but, hey, someone has to stand up to the evil ones in this world, and that's just what the Rev. Dubya and I did.

Did I say he was a great guy? Clever, eloquent, deep, prayerful, American (which is always great!) and, above all, I'm proud to say, my friend! Do I have any regrets about the way it's turned out? Well, all I can say is the Evil One is no longer with us. Doesn't that say it all?

The important thing is to move on.

CHAPTER SIX
My Cross

THROUGHOUT all my long and successful years at the vicarage, I had one terrible and persistent cross to bear.

This was my nextdoor neighbour, Mr Brown, our parish treasurer.

Don't get me wrong. Gordon is one of the nicest guys you could ever want to meet.

But even his best friends (if he has any, which I doubt) would have to admit that he can sometimes be a perverse, morose, devious, broody, two-faced, bullying, bi-polar,

totally incompetent weirdo.

The only real mistake I ever made was to step down as vicar and let Gordon have a chance at doing what he'd always wanted.

I guess I'm just too nice a guy, with too big a heart! I knew he'd be useless as vicar and he was even worse than I imagined.

The only reason I kept him on as treasurer for ten years was that, in the words of the Good Book, "Better a man inside the Church who pisseth out that one outside the Church that pisseth in" *(Proverbs 17.24)*.

Frankly, I don't mind telling you all that watching Gordon destroy everything I had worked for over so many years nearly turned me into a raging alcoholic.

At one point, I'll be honest, I was drinking two glasses of sherry a day!

Luckily, I am sufficiently strong-willed to have sorted myself out, unlike most of my former colleagues, such as Mr Campbell, Mrs Mowlam, Mrs Short and Mr Blunkett, not to mention all those who went mad without the aid of the bottle, like Mr Cook, Mr Clarke and our former Churchwarden, Mr Mandelson. Don't get me wrong, Peter is a great guy and a good friend, but he can be a smarmy, two-faced creep. And have you seen his memoirs? Totally unreadable, self-serving tosh. I mean, they read as if he's made everything up. They're already in the charity shop, by the way, at only 99p a copy. And I notice he didn't donate any royalties to the Poppy Appeal.

You know, the only one of my colleagues who stayed sane in those St Albion years was dear old Mr Prescott down at the Working Men's Club, whom we all enjoyed laughing at because he didn't know how to drink his tea and he couldn't speak properly and chased the barmaids around with a croquet mallet!

CHAPTER 94
The Way Ahead

SO where will my journey lead me next? It's pretty difficult when you've reached the top of the mountain, as I have, to know which peak to scale next.

What job could possibly be big enough for someone of my unrivalled experience, my communication skills and my unique record of public service?

Of course, I'm not interested in being Vicar of St Albion's again. My successor, the Rev. Cameron and his curate, the Rev. Clegg from the Liberal Democrat Reform Church, are doing a pretty good job, and certainly much better than that hopeless imbecile Mr Brown.

No, it's got to be bigger than anything I've done so far and maybe I'll have another of my dreams!

And maybe I'll dream that God appears to me (a great guy, by the way, although sometimes a bit too judgmental!) and he'll say, "Tony, I've been doing this job for millions of years and it's time for regime change! It's time to draw a line under me and let a younger man take over!".

And who knows, maybe my journey will go on and on and on. Forever and ever. Amen.

SUPERMODELS

KERBER

**In Memoriam
Tony Curtis, film actor**

So. Farewell
Then
Tony Curtis.

Hollywood legend.

Your most famous film
Was
Some Like It Hot.

Will it be hot
Where you are going?

I hope
Not.

E.J. Thribb (17½)

**In Memoriam
Paul, The Octopus**

So. Farewell
Then
Paul, the Psychic Octopus.

You predicted
All the winners
In the World Cup

But you did
Not predict your
Own demise.
Or did you?

Perhaps we shall
Never know.

Also. Farewell
The Emperor. The Great
Stag Of Exmoor.

Apparently you are
Dead.
Or not.

There is some
Confusion here.

E.J. Thribb (17½ arms)

**In Memoriam
Harry Wesley Coover Junior**

So. Farewell
Then
Harry Wesley Coover Junior
Inventor of Superglue.
You held
It all together
For 94
Years.

But now
At last
You have
Come unstuck.

E.J. Thribb (17½)

Downturn Abbey

Eye TV is proud to present the classic drama that the whole nation is talking about

The story so far… Agreeable, patrician aristocrat Lord Cameron has welcomed the gauche middle-class Nicholas Clegg into the family, to the horror of Dowager Dame Maggie who fears that Clegg will take over the estate, disinherit the rightful heiress, Lady George, and ruin everything.

There is trouble downstairs too, as the resentful footman, Hughes, plots and schemes under the watchful eye of the trusty butler, Cable, and thrifty housekeeper, Mrs Alexander.

⊹⇒ EPISODE 94 ⇐⊹

(The family are eating a lavish dinner in Downturn Abbey's sumptuous dining room)

Lord Cameron: You know, Nicholas, I expect all this seems all very stuffy and stuck-up and out of date to you, but you'll come round to our way of doing things and find that it is all for the best.

Nicholas Clegg: Thank you, Lord Cameron. You are most kind and I am beginning to see that, as you say, we are all in it together.

Lady George: Well, I think Clegg's the most frightful oik and absolutely ghastly and I don't see why we should all have to put up with him.

Lord Cameron: Really, George, not in front of the servants. You didn't hear any of that, did you, Cable?

Cable: No, your Lordship. Not a word.

Clegg: I had some ideas for the estate, Lord Cameron. I thought we could improve the housing for the workers and…

Dame Maggie: Workers have houses? Whatever next?

Clegg: It will require making some compromises…

Dame Maggie: And what is a compromise?

(The family all look embarrassed except Lady George who titters into her fish knife. Clegg nervously lights a cigarette)

Dame Maggie: Goodness me! Has he no manners? One never smokes until the ladies have retired.

Lord Cameron *(smiling)*: Well, yes, mother, perhaps it is a shame that some ladies didn't retire a bit earlier.

(Calm is restored by the wit and charming good sense of the enlightened Cameron. All relax. Suddenly there is a loud crash, as scheming footman Hughes spills a tureen of soup all over Lord Cameron's head)

Cameron: Aaargh!

Cable: You clumsy oaf, Hughes! I must apologise, your Lordship. I'll get Mrs Alexander to clean up the mess at once.

Cameron: No, no. It is of no consequence. Anyone can make a mistake.

Dame Maggie: Indeed. As you have so clearly demonstrated in your adoption of Mr Clegg!

(We hear dramatic, silly music)

To be continued…

⊹⇒ CAST IN FULL ⇐⊹

Lord Cameron	**Hugh Bonneville**
Nicholas Clegg	**Dan Stevens**
Cable	**Jim Carter**
Theresa May	**Penelope Wilton**
Dame Maggie	**Dame Maggie**

(That's enough cast. Ed.)

THE DAILY TELEGRAPH

Letters
to the Editor

SIR – I wonder how many viewers of ITV's Downton Castle were shocked as I was by the countless historical inaccuracies in what was an otherwise entertaining tale of ordinary everyday life in Edwardian England.

For instance when the butler, Mr. Carstairs, was seen laying the table for dinner in episode two, he placed the fish knives to the right of the soup spoons. This could never have happened in any well-ordered household of the type in which some of us were fortunate enough to spend our childhood.

As for the scullery maid addressing the Under-Housekeeper as "Mrs. Matthews" whilst wearing her cap! I can tell you such an offence would have resulted in instant dismissal and possibly death, and quite rightly so.

At least they got the jumbo jet right as it flew over the gathering of the Downton hunt in 1912, startling Lady Starborgling (an excellent performance, incidentally, by Dame Judi Mirren) in a reasonably authentic fashion.

Wake up BBC and try and stop getting things wrong!

Yours faithfully,

Sir Herbert Gusset

The Old Rehab Clinic For Distressed Gentlefolk, Notlong-on-the-Wagon, Nr. Barkworth, Somerset.

Births

MR JAMES AND MRS JOOLS OLIVER are delighted to announce the birth of a son, Luvly Jubbly, on 16th September, a brother for Wazzitup, Pukkatucka and Big Stylee Delish. Social Services have been informed.

"Is there a doctor on board?"

That All-Purpose Newspaper Editorial in Full

A T A TIME of national uncertainty it is not surprising that the nation turns for reassurance to the traditional world of Downton Abbey/Strictly Come Dancing/The X Factor. We all need comfort at this difficult time when the future seems so unsure and fraught with difficulties. No wonder we all of us sit down on Saturday/Sunday evening to wallow in the certainties of Edwardian costume drama/celebrity ballroom dancing/reality singing competition.

And haven't we all taken to our hearts the iconic national treasures that are the stars of the show? – the inimitable Dame Maggie Smith/Ann Widdecombe/Cheryl Cole.

Yes, there are carping critics who predictably claim that these shows are formulaic, cliché-ridden and designed to appeal to the lowest common denominator.

But that same criticism, it might be argued, could be levelled at all great works of art down the ages.

Could it not be said of Shakespeare himself that he "played to the gallery" with such characters as Lady Bracknell, Hercule Poirot and Inspector Morse (*is this right? Ed.*)

Such petty criticism is to miss the point entirely. There is a desire for escapism in all of us which Mr Fellowes/Bruce Forsyth/Simon Cowell understand all too well. Our thanks are due to them and their well-made concoctions for giving us such solid fare for the long winter nights ahead as we (*will this do?*)

"Isn't there a game we could both play, Keith?"

Opera Highlights

BBC Radio 3

Direct from La Scandala in Milan, *O Salome Mio!* by Berlusconi

Act One

Silvio, the Robber Baron, is in high spirits as he welcomes his entourage of beautiful girls to celebrate the anniversary of his divorce at the Palazzio Fornicatione. His eye is immediately taken by the curvaceous form of the virginal 17-year-old Bellyrina, *'La BungaBunga'*. He asks her to dance for him and she performs the seductive *'Dance of the Seven Thousand Euros'*. He sings the haunting aria *'La Donna*

Tell Anyone About This'. She is so moved by his song and his gift of a diamond necklace that she agrees to spend the night with the Robber Baron along with several other exotic dancers.

Act Two
The newspapers are full of Silvio's latest conquests but the Robber Baron laughs off the accusations. He sings the aria *'Sono Il Politico Ridiculoso' ('The Laughing Politician')* but an angry crowd beneath the window assembles throwing stones and crying for the Baron to resign. They sing the strident chorus *'Bastardo Corrupto' ('Is This Not An Appropriate Time For You To Resign Mr President, No Offence')*.

Will the Baron escape? Tune in tomorrow for our next opera *'Silvio Escapado' (The Escape of Silvio)*.

Wait 'til I tell Wikileaks about this

'WIKILEAK THREAT TO U.S. SECURITY,' CLAIMS GENERAL

*by Our Torture Staff **Keith Waterboard***

THOUSANDS of official U.S. documents leaked to the press today constitute a grave threat to the security of American troops in the field according to a Pentagon official.

Said senior army officer General Betraeus, "These documents giving evidence of U.S. involvement in the torture and killing of civilians are clearly detrimental to the U.S. army. If people find out what we have been up to, it could lead to a public outcry which would stop us getting up to the same thing again".

Donald Rumsfeld is 96.

RADIO 4 'FOUR LETTER WORD' SHOCK

*by Our Media Staff **James Very Naughtie** and **Andrew Marrksthesamemistake***

A BBC radio presenter yesterday astounded the nation by introducing the Secretary of State for Culture as Mr Jeremy Hunt.

Listeners around the country choked over their breakfast and thousands rang in to complain.

"This is not what I expect from the BBC," said one. "There could have been children listening – the least these presenters could do is get people's names right.

"Everyone knows that the correct pronunciation is Mr Jeremy Cunt."

The Hulture Secretary is 49.

Who will suffer the most from the introduction of £9,000 a year university tuition fees?

■ Liberal Democrats MPs hoping to be re-elected

■ Er…

■ That's it.

NOW IT'S WIDILEAKS

It's torture for everyone

19

THIS WEEK

BORIS JOHNSON

Do you have many spoons?

Cripes, well I can see what you are doing, you're trying to get me to admit I've got a lot of spoons and that at a time of national austerity it's a bit much for people like me to be so loaded spoon-wise…

No, I just wondered if…

Well it's a clear case of Non spoonibus quamquam pluribus quoque spoonabilis…

I'm sorry I don't follow…

We all know that YOU'VE got a lot of spoons, no doubt funded by the extremely well paid "Me and My Spoon Column".

I er…

I think the public would be very interested to know how many spoons YOU have got – a lot more than me and my hard working banker chums I would guess.

Has anything amusing…

Come on don't change the subject. Tell us, how many spoons have you got?

Is it true that you have moved your spoons into a separate flat down the road from your home…?

(Sadly at this point the interview was terminated)

NEXT WEEK: *Jimmy Choo, "Me and My Shoe"*

"Blimey, we'd better get his name down for one"

A message from His Holiness the Barmy Swami, Rev ARP Blair

(formerly Vicar of St Albion's)

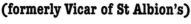

Drawing All
Faiths Together

Friends,

Can we take a moment to celebrate together the good news that my dear sister-in-law Lauren has embraced one of the world's great faiths? As believers, we at DAFT welcome any conversion of this kind which reaffirms for all of us the great bonds that join us together even when they drive us apart.

DAFT is a family of faiths and in my own personal family we now have a Roman Catholic, a practising alcoholic, a committed lawyer, and a Muslim! Not bad, eh?

And I think what Lauren's conversion teaches

us is that now that she is devoting her time to reading the Koran and wearing a silly headscarf, she will have less time to try and get herself in the papers by criticising me and pretending she cared about the Iraq war which was all a long time ago in any case and has no bearing on anything, particulary not my forthcoming address to the Board of Deputies Annual Dinner and Dance (only £3,000 per head, tickets still available).

Shalom, Salaam and good evening!! End of!

Rev. T. Blair
Chief Executive, D.A.F.T.

How Those Prisoners Will Vote

An exclusive Cut-Out-'n'-Keep Eye Guide to how the votes in Britain's gaols could swing the next election. A new poll shows the electoral leanings of different categories of prisoners.

MURDERERS	CONSERVATIVE	✔
FRAUDSTERS	CONSERVATIVE	✔
BURGLARS	CONSERVATIVE	✔
CANNABIS SMOKERS	LIB DEM	✔
BENEFIT FRAUD	LABOUR	✔
TV LICENCE EVASION	TORY (Chas. Moore)	✔
TERRORIST OFFENCES	RESPECT	✔
DRIVING WHITE VAN WITHOUT MOT, ROAD TAX, INSURANCE ETC.	BNP	✔
WAR CRIMES	NEW LABOUR (Tony Blair)	✔

Swing to Conservatives 82.3 percent

WHO ARE THEY – CAMERON'S 'TEAM VANITY'?

An Eye Guide to the PM's New Image Consultants on the Public Payroll

IZZY SPEARMINT-RHINO, 24, former fashion consultant at *The Lady*. Her job will be to advise SamCam on what to wear, with particular emphasis on what the weather's going to be like and whether she should put on a coat or take an umbrella. *(£179,000 pa)*

NURDI BALDI, 23, former guru of political social network site TwoFacebook. He will show Mr Cameron how to turn on the computer and look things up on Google, such as checking the weather before he goes out. *(£210,000 pa)*

MELISSA STARBORGLING, 19, former sixth-former at Cheltenham Ladies College. Melissa will use psychological profiles and Feng Shui techniques to advise the Cameron team on how to behave in difficult situations ie, when they are not sure what the weather is doing and don't know whether to wear a coat or take an umbrella. *(£370,000 pa) That's enough. Ed.*

● **The people who are making Cameron look bad by making him look good!!!**

DIARY

JULIAN FELLOWES

Why do people call one a snob? Snobs are socially insecure. I am not. For instance, I know instinctively how to hold a knife and fork. This is not to say I give a fig how others hold their knives and forks. It's entirely a matter for them. It's a free world. Let them hold their knives and forks in whatever ghastly little common way they want, for all I care!

If someone is comfortable holding their knife like a fountain pen (or that most vulgar of writing implements, the "felt tip") then all well and good. It's entirely up to him. One may always avert one's eyes. Just don't ask us to admire him for it! As Lord Grantham wisely observes to Carson on my televisual series, Downton Abbey:

Lord Grantham: It matters less how a man handles his fork, Carson, than how he handles the women folk.

Carson: Yes, my Lord.

Lord Grantham: After all, Carson, a fork is just a fork. But when all is said and done, a lady is a human being. Enough of this chit-chat, Carson: I fear it cannot be long before the First World War breaks out, and the world as we know it is altered for ever.

Carson: Will that be all, my Lord?

My new televisual series, Downton Abbey, has been the victim of predictable class-based criticism. Some people carp that it's snobbish. I'm sorry, but that's a typically lower-middle-class thing to say.

Others eke out their sad little existences by trying to catch us out on historical inaccuracies.

One of these oiks had the nerve to complain that a lady's maid would never have been heard whistling "Jumping Jack Flash" in 1912, as it is a tune by The Rolling Stones, first released a few years later. Another pointed out that they could see a Sky dish on the roof of Downton Abbey, even though aristocrats in those days watched little or no television.

And so the list of left-wing grievances drags on and on, a testament to typical Leninist bitterness. "A true Countess would never have been seen out hunting wearing hot-pants and a push-up bra" "Pot Noodles would not have been served for breakfast in a leading country house" "I clearly spotted the under-footman skateboarding to the village fete" "The electric toothbrush was not available until 1960" "No gentleman would ever appear before his valet in a posing-pouch". Jabber, jabber, jabber. Have these dreary little viewers nothing better to do with their time? Have they no understanding of that admittedly old fashioned concept – the imagination?

Ho-hum. I suppose such obsessive nit-picking helps occupy their tiny little left-wing minds. Thankfully, the better-educated among us treasure Downton Abbey for its telling aperçus, shining a bold new light on that most fascinating of eras.

I have a particular fondness for Lord Grantham, who proves, if proof be needed, that the English aristocracy enjoyed a remarkably warm-hearted relationship with those devoted to its service. In the second episode, I created this touching scene, in which he shows real compassion to his devoted butler, Mr Carson:

Carson: Might I have a word, my Lord?

Lord Grantham: Can't it wait, Carson? I am up to my neck in cufflinks, and my iPod is on the blink, dash it!

Carson: I do apologise, my lord. But it cannot wait. I wish to tender my resignation.

Lord Grantham: Your resignation! I say, Carson! Isn't this a trifle hasty? What, pray, is your reason?

Carson: I would rather not say, my Lord.

Lord Grantham: Look here, Carson. I insist that you tell me. Now, there's a good fellow. You at least owe me that.

Carson: It's about that chocolate cake, my Lord.

Lord Grantham: Ah yes. The chocolate cake.

Carson: One of the under-maids served it to Her Ladyship without providing the requisite spoon and fork. Consequently, the chocolate smeared itself all over Her Ladyship's face.

Lord Grantham: The poor darling looked like nothing so much as a Negro minstrel! Had not the Slave Trade been abolished by my good friend Lord Palmerston some fifty years ago, my wife would might been chained to an oar of a slave ship and rowing herself to the West Indies, even as we speak, Carson!

Carson: I shall never forgive myself, My Lord. And for that reason, I wish to tender my resignation.

Lord Grantham (tenderly): I won't hear of it, Carson. We must let bygones be bygones. Far better that I should dock six months wages from your salary and forget all about it.

Carson (discreetly wiping away tears of joy): I promise you, My Lord, you shall never regret your decision!

Lord Grantham: It behoves the well-born to overlook the minor misdemeanours of those less intelligent than themselves, Carson. And, with poor Archduke Franz Ferdinand shortly to be shot, and the First World War looming, who can say what the future will hold?

Carson: Yes, my Lord. Will that be all, my Lord?

As told to CRAIG BROWN

Let's Parlez Franglais!

Numéro 94

Sur Le Joint Command Aircraft Carrier, HMS Napoleon Bonaparte

Admiral Anglais: Hello, matelot!

Admiral Français: Bonjour, sailor!

Admiral Anglais: Vive l'entente cordiale!

Admiral Français: Vive la Frangleterre!

Admiral Anglais: C'est un très good idea, n'est-ce pas, cette sharing de l'aircraft carrier?

Admiral Français: Absolument! Pour les incidents internationaux.

Admiral Anglais: Comme les Falklands!

Admiral Français: Er... peut-être not! En cette case, nous devons supporter les Argies et flogger them nos exocet missiles pour attaquer **this** ship... er...

Admiral Anglais: Typical grenouilles!

Admiral Français: Rosbifs typiques!

Admiral Anglais: Goodbye, matelot!

Admiral Français: Au revoir, sailor!

© Le late Kilometres Kington 2010.

CAMERON AND SARKOZY AGREE HISTORIC DEAL TO SHARE WIVES

"If you don't give in, we'll quit"

Literary characters in their retirement

No 94. Pussy Galore

Daily Mail

WILL ROYAL WEDDING SAVE BRITAIN'S ECONOMY?

House prices tipped to rocket as Wills weds

by Our Entire Business Staff **Sue Veneer** and **Ivor TeaTowel**

CITY analysts were today hailing the planned Royal Wedding as the miracle that will lift Britain's economy out of recession and turn us once again into the workshop of the world.

Said one City expert, "I predict that Britain will return to its rightful place as the powerhouse of manufacturing, as industry gears up to produce billions of mugs, plates, spoons, tea towels, balloons, commemorative trouser presses and Wills and Kate party poppers, produced by the Middleton Party Popper Co."

"Within twelve months," he went on, "we can expect to see Britain surging ahead of China as the world's leading *(cont. p. 94)*

 How They Are Related

Wills the Conqueror	Old King Cole
Wills and Mary	Arthur Scargill
Wills Hakespeare	Pit the Elder
W.D. and H.O. Wills	T'Pit the Younger
Kaiser Wills Helm	Sir Humphry Davy
Wills & Boon	D.H. Lawrence
The Bishop of Wills Den	Cole Porter
H.G. Wills	John Coal
A.N. Wills	Ken Collier
Wills Elf	Morris Miner
Just Wills	Glenda Slagg Heap
Wills Windsor	**Kate Middleclass**

What shall I give them as a present?

The throne?

GLENDA SLAGG

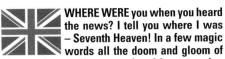

She's the Royal Lady-in-Writing!?! (Geddit).

ROYAL ENGAGEMENT SPECIAL

WHERE WERE you when you heard the news? I tell you where I was – Seventh Heaven! In a few magic words all the doom and gloom of Cameron's cuts disappeared and it was spring again!!! And I tell you for why Mister in case you've been on Mars for the last week! Our handsome Prince is marrying his childhood sweetheart! Wills 'n' Kate – Doesn't it sound great! That's Glenda's little poem (eat your heart out Carol Ann Duffy!). Pass me the Kleenex someone, Glenda needs another little weep!!?

■ **FOR CRYING** out loud can't everyone put a sock in it!! I'm talking about the flood of sentimental drivel that's going to drown us all! So Prince Wills is getting hitched to some girl he met at a party years ago! Who cares??? I DON'T WANT TO READ ABOUT IT!!! Geddit!!? "Will and Kate. They're the ones I hate". Glenda's little poem – Eat your heart out Andrew Motion! Pass me the sickbag someone, Glenda needs to throw up again!

■ **MRS MIDDLETON?** That's Kate's Mum to you Mister! Dunchajuslover?!? With her skin tight jeans and to-die-for-hair she's got CLASS written all over her and I don't mean Middle!?! (Geddit?!). Ok, so she used to be an air hostess. But it's her daughter who has landed on her feet!! Good for you Mrs Mmmm!!!!!

■ **MRS MIDDLETON** – Mrs Mutton-ton-dressed-as-lamb more like!? Skin tight jeans at your age? And which bottle did you get that hair colour from Ducky – cos you ain't fooling none of us! Whydoncha go back to being a trolley dolly love

and when you hear them say "Doors to Manual" jump out!?! No offence, Ma'am!

■ **READ WHAT** the Batty Bishop of Willesden said about the nation's favourite couple??? He gives them seven years!!!! What a disgrace!?!! I thought Bishops were all in favour of marriage – or is that only to each other?!? Take a tip from Auntie Glenda – Don't show your Facebook round here Bishop Broad-Bent (Geddit?!) or you'll get your crook shoved where the sun doesn't shine!! Only you might enjoy that *(That's enough, Ed.)*

■ **HATS AND MITRES** off to the Brave Bishop of Willesden who tells it like it is!? Kate and Wills?? "Shallow Celebrities"??, "National Celebration"???, "Nauseating Tosh"??!?. Yes, it needs a Man of God to put us on the Straight and Narrow, "So thank the Lord for Bishop Pete. He's not scared to put his views on a Tweet". Glenda's little Thought for the Day – Eat your heart out Rabbi Blue!

■ **HERE THEY ARE** – Glenda's Best Men (Geddit!?!!)!?!

● **Mr Middleton** – Kate's Dishy Dad! Come round to my party Michael with some Poppers and things will really go with a bang!

● **Tom Bradby** – ITN's Royal-Interviewer-in-Waiting! I like a bit of soft soap now and again?!??! (Geddit?!?)

● **Gary Goldsmith** – He's Kate's Hunky Uncle with the Love Nest in Ibiza. –When do I get my invite to Villa Bang Bang Gary? I can't Waity! (Geddit??!!)

Byeee!!

"Apparently, our invasion of Britain was illegal – how about yours?"

EXCLUSIVE TO THE DAILY TELEGRAPH

An Open Letter to Allison Pearson from

Kate Middleton

Dear Allison,

Firstly, may I congratulate you on your new column in the Daily Telegraph. You've waited a long time for this role and you've had your share of heartache when your relationship with the Daily Mail broke down. But you've risen above it; you've braved all those who sneered at your humble middle-class background and said that you weren't really up to the job on the Telegraph. They very unkindly called you "Allison Drearson", "Allison Pearshaped" and, worst of all, "Polly Filler"!

But you've come through it all and I wish you every happiness with the Daily Telegraph. It's going to be tough – there are going to be letters from people saying, "What's the point of Allison Pearson?", "Why doesn't she get a proper job?" and "Can she stop writing patronising open letters to people she doesn't know in which she recycles all the old clippings and pretends to be caring?"

And of course you are going to be compared to your predecessor, the Princess of columnists, the saintly Glenda Slagg.

But don't worry, Allison, although she shone like the brightest of stars, I am confident that you can be even worse than her.

Yours sincerely,

Kate Middleton

THE DAILY CHAIN MAIL

Friday 6 January 1533

Royal Marriage 'Won't Last Seven Years', Says Bishop

by Our Fawning Correspondent Rick Spittle

ONE OF England's leading bishops has launched an astonishing rant about the forthcoming marriage between King Henry VIII and his beautiful bride-to-be, Anne Boleyn. Thomas Cranmer, a senior bishop, has written an article in his Commonplace-book denouncing the Royal Family

as a bunch of tyrants, and criticising the media for producing reams of 'fawning deferential nonsense'. Even more insanely, he criticises the King's FAMILY, saying it's full of 'broken marriages and philanderers'.

We would like to make perfectly clear where our allegiances lie. We can only

hope that our glorious king executes the bishop as soon as possible.

On Other Pages

● 'You've never had it so good', minister tells starving peasants

● Ruinously expensive wars overseas continue

● King executes wife

The Secret DIARY OF SIR JOHN MAJOR KG aged 97¾

It gives me not inconsiderable pleasure to say that Mr Cameron's new coalition is in my judgment the greatest item since the sliced bread that my wife Norman puts in the toaster each morning to accompany my breakfast of Golden Grahams. Oh yes.

"Perhaps they should rename these Golden Davids", I said to her, "Or possibly Golden Nicks as a sign of how successful the two leaders have been."

I took Norman's silence as an indication of how much she had appreciated my not unamusing observation. So I continued to explain to her my reasons for applauding Mr Cameron in such no small measure.

"He has tamed the Tories. He has got rid of the Bastards," I told her. "I used to write their names in books and underline them in red biro but I could never get rid of them. I have often wondered why".

"I can tell you," Norman replied. "It is because you were too busy forming a coalition with Mrs Curry!" She then poured hot water over my trousers, missing my coffee cup by a not inconsiderable distance, again showing she has little grasp of either the kettle or contemporary politics. Oh no.

The Irish Nursery Times

Price €1 or 300 pints of Guinness

Support Irish in need, says Sir Terry Wogan

···· Friday, November 25, 2010 ····

LEPRECHAUNS DISCOVER 'CROCK OF SHIT AT END OF RAINBOW'

by Our Dublin Correspondent **Liffey Purves**

THE Little People were said to be furious today when the promised Crock of Gold turned out to be nothing more than a "crock of shit".

Said the Chief Leprechaun, Biffo Cowen, "We had been told that we would find untold wealth if we simply put all the money we had made making shoes into property and banking."

He continued, "Now when we get to the end of the rainbow we find a man from

Brussels telling us we owe him billions of euros.

"It's a disgrace to be sure and all and all."

Full story and pics p94

"From this point you can see mummy in a car with another man"

THE Sun SAYS

IT'S THE BBC WOT LOST IT!

Forget Sepp Blatter! Forget the brown envelopes stuffed with roubles! Forget the shady sheikh with his sack of shekels! No, the real villain of the piece is sitting right here on our own front doorstep.

It's the BBC! The Bid Bashing Corporation which blew our world-beating bid out of the water with a load of lies that told the truth about what goes on behind closed doors at Fifa!

Trust the pinkos at Panorama to put the boot in on the day of decision – when *all* the signs pointed to an England win!!

What happened to pride? What happened to patriotism? What happened to pride and patriotism?

We say it is time the BBC was shut down for good and for Sky Sport to cover the World Cup exclusively from now until the end of time. And time added on. Three cheers for Mr Murdoch!

ME AND MY SPOON

THIS WEEK

CHRIS MOYLES

Do you have a favourite spoon?

Don't talk to me about spoons. The bloody BBC haven't given me any spoons for bloody ages. What bastards! You'd think they would show me some respect after all I've done for them, but no, not one bloody spoon – does Terry Wogan get treated like this? No, he's got as many spoons as he wants. Chris Evans? Spoons coming out of his arse... But me? Nothing. Does Moylesy get a single bloody teaspoon to stir his coffee on the most popular breakfast show in the history of the galaxy? No.

But surely you have quite a lot of spoons already? I've seen a figure quoted of hundreds of thousands of spoons.

I'm not talking about what I've got, dickhead. I'm talking about what I want now. And Moylesy wants spoons.

But the BBC have promised you even more spoons, haven't they?

You're not listening, are you, shit for brains? It's not about *spoons*, it's about *respect*. Respecting the man who saved Radio One singlehandedly. Respecting the biggest star in British Broadcasting today.

Has anything amusing ever happened on your radio show?

No.

NEXT WEEK: *Me and My Irons with Jeremy Irons.*

REALITY SHOW

"Is your use of the word 'journey' really necessary?"

24

THOSE WIKILEAKS IN FULL

World politics was rocked to its foundations yesterday by the most sensational revelations ever revealed by anyone in the history of the world.

HERE are some of the most amazing verdicts on world figures by US diplomats, as disclosed in the two billion emails from US embassies which were leaked to every newspaper in the world last night and caused the biggest political embarrassment ever known in the history of the planet *(You've done this. Ed.)*

President Karzai of Afghanistan "Corrupt, shifty, incompetent"

President Sarkozy of France "Vain, silly, French"

Prime Minister Berlusconi of Italy "Sex mad, corrupt, sex mad"

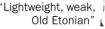
Prime Minister David Cameron of England "Lightweight, weak, Old Etonian"

Chancellor George Osborne of England "Lightweight, weak, not Old Etonian"

Prime Minister Ahmadinejacket of Iran "Mad, Moslem, bearded lunatic"

Supreme Leader King Jong-II of North Korea "Mad, Communist, clean-shaven lunatic"

His Holiness Pope Benedict XVI "Catholic"

More WikiLeaks in full 2-94

TAP TAP TAP

HAN THINKS LUKE IS A USELESS JEDI... MORE INFO SOON!!

WookieLeaks

RGJ

NHS HOW TO BOOK A VISIT TO YOUR LOCAL DOCTOR

❏ **Call NHS Direct's non emergency number**

❏ **Be redirected to a call centre in Bangalore**

❏ **Carefully detail your symptoms to the cheery Indian call centre worker who claims his name is Steve and keeps mentioning the score in the Arsenal verses Man U game at the weekend for no obvious reason**

❏ **Receive an appointment at 9am on Tuesday with a doctor three hundred miles from your home**

❏ **Try and explain to the cheery call centre worker that you need an appointment closer to your home**

❏ **Raise your voice as the call centre worker insists his computer tells him that Abu Dhabi is in Gloucestershire**

❏ **Scream that you want a different appointment**

❏ **Receive a warning that screaming and shouting can result in high blood pressure**

❏ **Be given a new appointment with a doctor in Dubrovnik for high blood pressure**

❏ **Hang up**

❏ **Phone BUPA**

WIDDILEAKS OUTRAGE GROWS

by Our Leak Staff **Jonathan Leake**

THERE was mounting embarrassment throughout the world this week when yet another picture of Ann Widdecombe found its way into the Daily Telegraph.

The picture is the most damaging to date, and is obviously

leaked from the Strictly Come Dancing press office.

It reveals Ann Widdecombe to be someone who "would wear a gingham dress, carry a dog and try and look like Dorothy from The Wizard of Oz".

Said a shocked WiddiLeak analyst, "This is just the latest in a huge dump of Widdi material, which has sent shockwaves through the world. Although it may not appear to tell us anything." He continued, "It does confirm what we already suspected, ie Ann Widdecombe needs to be stopped before it is too late."

The condom split – and there was a Wikileak!

Names of the year

Sir, As is customary at this time of the year, I have compiled a list of the most popular names recorded in your "births" column during the past 12 months:

Boys	**Girls**
1. Wills	Kate
2. Dave	SamCam
3. Nick	Gaga
4. Wiki	Widdy
5. Iain Duncan-Smith	Vuvuzela
6. Mr Potato Head	Mrs Potato Head
7. Wagner	Dannii
8. Downton	Abii
9. Kim Jong-il	Baroness Warzi
10. Assange	(Name withheld for legal reasons)

POPE BENEDICT THE CUMBERPATCH, (XVI)
The Old Vatican, Italy.

STRANGE NOISE DISTURBS SPANISH PEASANTS

by Our Science Staff **Spinny Gonzalez**

SPANISH peasants in the sleepy village of El Marmito were today woken from their siesta by subterranean rumblings, which have baffled seismologists.

Said one, "The epicentre appears to be the final resting place of the man they called Don Fishpasto, the legendary Sir Jammy Goldfish himself."

Achtung!

The rumblings began when the late financier's daughter, Jemima Puddleduck, appeared on television to proclaim her support for the Wikileaks founder Julian Assange.

Said the seismologist, "It was the exact moment when she offered some of the JamPaste millions as bail for Mr Assange that the mysterious noises started. Then when she declared her belief in the importance of free speech and the leaking of confidential information, the sound got louder and louder until it was deafening.

Talbot Story

"We now believe that the underground disturbances were caused by an object in a box revolving or spinning furiously."

Said one villager, Lord Lucan, "You haven't seen me, right."

● **Full story, page 94**

STUDENT RIOTS

'A TRIUMPH FOR MODERN POLICING'
Knacker's Shock Claim

by Our Police Staff **P.C. World**

INSPECTOR 'Knacker of the Yard' Knacker today defended police tactics in handling the recent protests over university fees.

Said Knacker, "The boys in blue walk a very delicate tightrope between the right of the individual to express their opinion in a democratic society and the right of my lads to hit them over the head with their batons."

Knacker went on to defend his use of the controversial "kettling" strategy.

"People do not understand," he said, "how kettling works. What happens is that my lads form a ring around the students, so they cannot get out except through a small aperture akin to the spout of a traditional household kettle.

"Things then get a bit hot, the students boil over and start letting off steam, at which point we can start hitting them over the head with the batons."

On Other Pages

Fifteen letters from angry middle-class parents, protesting that their children were not permitted to go to the toilet for half an hour, even though they went to a good school and spoke very politely to the officers involved 24

You're being poked, darling!

Chance would be a fine thing

THE ALTERNATIVE VOICE

Dave (David) Fotherington Spart Co-Chair of Students Against The Fascist Coalition And Death to Clegg Now Collective (Notting Hill)

It is totally and utterly sickening for the rightwing reactionary neo-con media to try and caricature the grass roots workers and students protests against the genocidal cuts as nothing more than a collection of upper middle class drop outs playing at revolution er… whereas the fact that er… some of us went to Marlborough and Uppingham has absolutely nothing to do with anything nor does the fact that my Dad is a barrister and Jamie's Mum works for a Hedge Fund but er… basically, Dad, if you are reading this could you pay my fine because I'm a bit short and I was hoping to go skiing over Xmas with Emma and Isabel … er as I was saying it is totally and utterly nauseating to observe the industrial-military complex allying itself with the (cont. p.94)

Court Circular

10 December, 2010

Today His Royal Highness the Prince of Wales and the Duchess of Cornwall will attend the Royal Variety Performance at the London Palladium. They will be met in Regent Street by the following representatives of the student anarchist community:

The Hon. Charlie Ricketson-Smythe (History of Art, Durham). **Lady Lobelia Kropotkin** (Social Sciences and Photography, University of Wolverhampton, formerly West Midland Polytechnic). **Anne Archist** (Theology and Golf Course Management, Guildford Sixth Form College).

The Royal couple will be presented with a can of white paint and a stick through the window, to commemorate their historic visit to the scene of the Tuition Fees Riot.

PROCESSION
1st Rolls Royce
HRH Prince of Wales and the Duchy of Original

2nd Police car
Inspector Clueless (Royal Protection Unit) accompanied by armed officers of the RPU including Sgt. X, PC. Y, and WPC. Z.

1st Rickshaw
Mr Sanjiv Samosa (Driver); Mr and Mrs Brad and Betty Grossburger from Idaho (who were trying to get to *Les Misérables*)

(That's enough. Ed.)

LORD Gnome

IT IS hard to describe my outrage at the recent scenes of lawlessness in some of my high street outlets – British Gnome Stores, Top Dog, Sweat Shop and other prestigious retail boutiques that come under the Arsholia umbrella.

At a time of year when shoppers are exercising their democratic right to give me money, it is little short of scandalous that hoodlums claiming to be "protestors" can disrupt this vital festive service to consumers.

I have been accused by these anarchists and terrorists of "avoiding taxes". What nonsense! I pay my taxes just like everybody else. The fact that my wife receives my entire fortune whilst resident on the remote island of St Evadia in the Bahamas is neither here nor there – although as it happens all the money is **there** and I am **here**.

But surely at this time of year we can agree to put aside our differences and come together in the spirit of harmony? I therefore welcome these misguided young people into my stores where I would like to offer them the following incredible pre Xmas bargains:

● Pair Jeans; £2.10 ● Pair Trainers: £1.10 ● T-Shirt bearing logo "Made by a Four Year Old": 9p

Lord Gnome,
c/o Lady Gnome,
The Old Slavery,
St. Evadia,
The Bahamas.

I'LL PUT THE KETTLE ON

POLICE

MORE STUDENT PROTESTS

ROBERT THOMPSON

KNACKER IN CONFUSION OVER 'DEMANDS FOR CANNON'

by Our Armed Response Staff **Polly Kettle** and **Cannon Law**

A HUGE row has erupted over the Met's demands that police should be better equipped to cope with the current wave of student protests.

Inspector Knacker of the Metropolitan Police said last night, "Under current deployment policies, my lads have nothing to fall back on in protecting themselves except standard issue low-level weaponry such as .45 magnums, AK47s and Hechler & Koch sub-machine guns.

"In face of the modern style of protest, carried out by radicalised and militarised members of the student anarchist community, some as old as 16, these are wholly inadequate."

"What we need are proper weapons, eg cannon, mortars, long-range artillery and air-to-ground missiles fired by aerial drones controlled from Texas."

Water Cannon on the brain

Hardly had Inspector Knacker spoken, however, than he issued a clarification statement. "When I called for the Met to be issued with low-yield nuclear weapons," he said, "my remarks were taken out of context."

"What I actually said was we should lay landmines around Whitehall and Parliament Square to allow these students to engage in peaceful democratic protest without any need for police to hit them over their heads with batons."

THE LIFE OF LADY ANTONIA FRASER

by Mary Queen of Scots

THE EYE is proud to publish an extract from the Historical Biography of the Year – which has become an international best-seller even before it has been published.

Chapter 94

The beautiful widowed Lady Antonia, still dressed in black, lifted her veil to consider the morning's post. Outside a few flakes of snow fell mournfully on the rooftops of Ladbroke Grove.

She looked at the welcome mat on which her late husband the beloved Harold Pinter, the Shakespeare of his day, had written in black paint "Fuck Off".

And there sitting on the mat she espied what was unmistakably a letter from Buckingham Palace.

Her heart leapt as she tore open the Royal Seal and read the beautiful copperplate handwriting of Her Majesty the Queen of England herself.

NOT A CIRCULAR

Dear Mrs Pinter of Ladbroke Grove,

You, Mrs Pinter of Ladbroke Grove, have been given a unique opportunity to win a prize of a Dame of the British Empire Award. All you have to do, Mrs Pinter of Ladbroke Grove, is to tick the box marked "YES" and our representatives will contact you with the details of how to claim your prize.

Yours faithfully,
Russell Twisk
(Her Majesty's Honours Secretary on Secondment from the Reader's Digest).

As she grasped the letter tightly to her bosom, her only thought was not for herself but for her late beloved Harold.

She seemed to hear his voice from far away, yet still as distinct and powerful as it had been in life. "Taking a fucking gong from the fucking Tories? They should cut your fucking head off."

© *Mary Queen of Scots 2010*

VIEWERS COMPLAIN OVER 'DISGUSTING' X-FACTOR FINAL

by Our Showbiz Staff **Rhiannothingon**

THE ITV switchboards were jammed after the X Factor final last week by angry members of the public who were ringing in to complain about the "shocking display of semi-naked greed".

Said one viewer, "It was well before the watershed and we were watching with our impressionable children when suddenly on screen came this shameless and frankly revolting spectacle of sleazy moneymaking.

"Everything was about cheques! Cheques, cheques, cheques, wherever you looked! For the record company, for the film company, for ITV, for Simon Cowell."

Another viewer agreed, saying, "I do not want to watch grown men and women begging me to phone up and give them 35p a minute and considerably more if you are calling from a mobile phone.

"It's obscene and, frankly, this squalid exhibition of tacky commercialism spoiled my enjoyment of the otherwise excellent raunchy lesbian dance routine, featuring Christina Aguilera in a bordello, wearing a basque and fishnet stockings. I hope ITV are ashamed of themselves."

● Were you shocked by the X Factor? If so, call Private Eye now at 089897573217562 and register your protest!
● Calls charged at 94p a second (£9.40 for mobile phones)

"I hate what you're turning into, Phil!"

DANGEROUS JUDGE MUST BE PUT DOWN
Court's Savage Ruling

by Our Legal Staff **JOSHUA ROZENBEARD**

A HIGH Court judge who got "out of control" and went on the rampage was ordered to be put down yesterday.

The female judge, Beatrice, described by her owner as a "pedigree lawyer" and by the victim as "a prize bitch", reduced the Law Courts to chaos by running amok, barking four-letter words in all directions and snarling at court officials.

Despite the defence's plea that Beatrice was normally "very well behaved" and was "good with children", the court ordered the judge to be destroyed.

"It is very sad," said a spokesman, "but there is a health and safety issue here. If people are going to have High Court judges, they must be properly trained and kept under tight control at all times."

Judge Beatrice Bolton is 94 (seven dog years).

PLEASE
RESPECT OUR
PRIVACY

ROGER LATHAM

A Doctor Writes

AS A GP I am often asked, "Doctor would you like to run the NHS?".

The short answer is "no" it's incredibly difficult and I have no qualifications for running such a vast organisation.

The long answer however is "Ok I might be persuaded particularly if you make it worth my while".

What happens is that the patient or Prime Minister, as he is called, comes to me with a serious medical problem which is technically know as *Budgetentitis Deficitissimus Normalis.*

The symptoms are a chronic lack of money combined with feelings of panic and depression.

Normally I would just refer him to a specialist at the Hospital who would have a better grasp of the best treatment for his condition.

But if patient is determined for me as a GP to take charge of his case then I have no choice but to agree and to submit my invoice in due course.
© *A. Doctor, The British Medical Journal, 2011.*

BLANKET OF INCOMPETENCE COVERS UK

by Our Weather Staff **Jon Snow**

BRITAIN ground to a halt yesterday beneath a thick layer of idiocy, with some parts of the country reporting record levels of stupidity.

Said one observer, "It has come as a real shock. People woke up in the morning to find that the entire country was buried in huge drifts of sheer incompetence.

"Nothing worked, no-one could go anywhere or do anything, and no-one knew why."

Complete Shite Out

"It was horrific. It will take weeks to clear this up or not because we probably won't be able to."

On other pages

■ *Readers' incompetence pictures* **2-94**

DIARY

TINA BROWN

It may have taken Kate eighteen years to hook William, but she's sure as hell not gonna let him skedaddle now – or not until she's reeled him in, hit him over the head, stuffed him into her poacher's bag, taken him home, filleted and skinned him, and given his boneless, headless corpse to lower-class EastEnder Mummy Middleton to fry in batter and serve wrapped in yesterday's newspaper with chips and catsup.

To the power-hungry Queen Elizabeth of England the news of the Royal engagement has come like a bolt from the blue. A senior Royal insider tells me her first reaction was to slam her expensively-jewelled fist down on the Louis Quatorze Royal Coffee Table and scream, "Why the f*** wasn't I told?" 'til she was blue in the face as well as the blood.

Three weeks after the announcement, and Beth's still mad as hell. Beneath her demure exterior, she's always been cash-fixated, and she sure as hell doesn't want any two-bit commoner chewing her way through the family fortune.

But for now, she's all sweetness 'n' light – at least in public. When British TV shows Kate and the Queen out on the town together, taking in a show or high-stooling it with a fancy cocktail at the newly-opened American Bar at London's newly-refurbed Claridge's Hotel, viewers truly can't tell there's a rift between them as big as the Grand Canyon, the US of A's historic national landmark.

A highly placed source in royal circles whispers in my ear over a $325 meal at London's fashionable Ritz Hotel that flame-haired Fergie – former wife of jug-eared Prince Edward – is hell-bent on gate-crashing the Royal nuptials in May.

And her plan is even more audacious than that. While glossy-haired Royal Bride Kate loiters in the piss-elegant boudoir of St Paul's – the antique retro-chic church they've power-hired for the big day – Fergie plans to leap on her, gag her, throw a king-size sack over her head and bundle her into the vestibule. Then she'll switch her own gaudy XXL rags for Kate's stunning sexy lycra hey-big-boys-come-'n'-get-me all-in-one wedding gown and with a veil over her face Fergie will stride up that aisle like there's no tomorrow.

Only when Prince Wills has said his I-do's and pulls the veil off her freckle-spattered head will he realise that he's married the wrong broad – but by then it'll be too late: Princess Fergie will have got her claws into the British throne, and there'll be nothing any true blue-blood can do about it.

So what made the self-styled Prince of Hearts fall under the spell of Gorbals-educated any-old-iron-any-old-iron-any-any-any-old-iron gorblimey songbird Kate Middleton?

For an answer to that tragic question, you have to travel back to that tragic night when tragic Princess Di crashed to her tragic death with tragic Dodi on the paparazzi-thronged underpasses of the tragic ancient city of Rome, current home of Ben, top billionaire former Nazi celebrity Pope.

It is a closely-guarded secret that I was with Dodi and Di in the back of their stretch limo that tragic night but managed to hurl myself out the window and onto the back of a passing moped in the nick of time. But while the rest of the world lost a Princess that night, Wills lost more than a Princess: he lost a mom.

The British nation was sent into a tail-spin of grief from which it never recovered. Ever since, Britain's ruling class – chaired by top finger-pointing aristo Lord Sugar – has been hell-bent on reviving national morale by masterminding a Royal marriage. Having hand-picked Kate from a shortlist of 10, bristle-based Sugar called in London high-flier Prince William and issued him with the order to marry her – or else.

The result? The British people are merry once more, with up to 60 million loyal maidens and serfs donning bells and straw hats to dance lustily around hastily-erected maypoles to the music of recently-reformed Take That on their trademark village greens. Such merriment has struck long-term rival Ireland a bitter blow, causing it to take to the bottle and spiral into mega-debt, and thrusting Romeo Italian premier Silvio Berlusconi, spitting with jealousy, has secretly offered flaxen-haired Katie over a million pesetas for a night of passion at his Vatican love-nest. All of which has made furious Queen Elizabeth vow revenge – and it's Katie who'll be taking the flak.

To keep updated, watch this mega-space.

As told to CRAIG BROWN

"AND THE DISH RAN AWAY WITH THE SPOON" WHAT'S A DISH? WHAT'S A SPOON? WHAT'S "RAN"?

NURSERY RHYMES

K.J.Lamb

GLENDA SLAGG

Fleet Street's Very Own Anti-Freeze!!!!

■ DIDN'T it bring a li'l tear to your eye? A baby born on Christmas Day – and by immaculate conception too! No, not in Bethlehem, stoopid, but in Los Angeles. And the only star involved was the proud father, our very own Sir Elton John!!?!! No wonder baby Zachary, the Son of David (geddit???) and Elton looked so happy!!!?! What better start could any little babby have in life than to have two such doting parents??!? And, unlike Mary and Joseph, they're even married!!?! So raise your glasses everybody, and sing "Hallelujah" to the newborn King of Showbiz!!!!

■ SIR ELTON – doesn't it make you sick???! So gay grandad and his boring boyfriend have bought a baby as a Christmas present to themselves!!! What do they think they're playing at???! Elton will be 100 before the toddler learns how to call him "Daddy"!?!!!?! And who's the poor little mite meant to call "Mummy" in this seedy set-up??!? The test tube??!? The spatula??!?? Liz Hurley??!? *(Is this right? Ed.)* What a sick parody of the Biblical Christmas story!!! Three Kings??!? Two old queens, more like!!?!? Yes, the kid may have plenty of gold showered on him, but there's more to bringing up a kid than wearing gold underpants and dancing around like a lunatic!!?! Isn't it time the social workers took a closer look at Zachary Jackson Levon Furnish-John???!? Or should that be "Baby Z"??!? Urgggghhh!!! All together now – "Unto us a child is bought". Geddit???!?

■ HERE THEY ARE – Glenda's Wicked Winter Warmers!?!

● Ricky Ponting – he may be a loser on the field, but he can make a big score round at my place any time (and bring your baggy green cap, cobber!!!).

● Julian Assange – Mr Weetabix to you *(surely WikiLeaks??!!? Ed.)* Here's one gal who won't try to get you arrested as soon as it's over!!!?! (Geddit, Mr Twice-a-night??!??)

● Simon Hughes – the Lib Dems' Mr Gay. Surely you can do a u-turn on that one as well, Hughsie. Mmmm!!!!

Byeee!!

An uncut version of this column can be seen at our website on www.philcyberspace.com

How many pounds did Zack weigh in at?

350,000 plus vat

ME AND MY SPOON

PRINCE ANDREW

Do you have a favourite spoon?

Typical. You f***ing journalists are always sticking your f***ing noses into things that are none of your business.

I just wondered if you had a favourite spoon?

Look, this is an idiotic investigation and it should be dropped. Let's just get on with promoting British spoons, shall we? That is my job, which is why I fly all over the world, often in a helicopter, meeting a lot of people and playing a lot of golf.

Do spoons play a prominent role in your life?

What's the matter? Are you from the Daily British Guardian or something? I said I do this God-awful job for nothing, and I don't get paid – not even in spoons. I must be bloody mad.

Has anything amusing ever happened to you in connection with a spoon?

This Kazakh bloke once bought a spoon off me for £15 million. Bloody funny, since it wasn't worth more than a fiver and don't quote me for f***'s sake..

NEXT WEEK: *Me and My Dinner Jacket with President Ahmadinejacket*

From The Message Boards

Members of the online community respond to the major issues of the day...

Protect doggers say police chiefs

The new guidance orders the protection of those cottaging, cruising or dogging because they can suffer "post traumatic stress and depression" if they are abused by the public. It calls this "managing public sex environments". Being ex-job myself I remember managing these environments by sitting on top of cubicles in public conveniences for hours on end. There was no room for members of the public to spectate, so the problem of heckling and abuse never arose. Life was more civilised back then. – *Brian*

i was up the park and i suddly took of my trouser's juss to see wat it felt like? only i dint have any pant's on that day i must of fergot them? it wernt doging "BUT" peple shout thing's and theres grafitie on the bus stop it say's kev is a perv and their's a disgustin picteur of me and i complane in case kid's and old peple see it "BUT" its stil their ☺ BE WARND TRAUMA ACTIALY REALY HAPENS AND ITS NOT FUNY IF ITS YOU – *hAnsolo*

My wife and I have many hobbies, including real ale, non-league football and dogging. What they all have in common is great camaraderie and terrific banter. One night we were watching an old dear going at it with a young chap in a van. Look at those old bangers, I said to the bloke next to me, referring to some abandoned cars near by. Unfortunately he was the lady's husband and thought I was talking about her "thruppnies", which were a bit rough! Anyway, he saw the funny side in the end, and we shared our sandwiches and some coffee from his thermos. Turned out he was an off-duty copper and he reckoned there are quite a few doggers in the force. – *Dogger_Bank*

I agree: the dogging scene is nothing like the sleazy reports in the media. As our official website states: "Go prepared for safe sex" and "Most of all, make sure everyone is happy and having fun." Although dogging is defined as a "predominantly British activity" we are keen to encourage more participation among foreigners and minorities, especially Muslims. – *Dogsbody*

Anyone noticed how the gay policemen and their surrogate "son" are keeping very quiet about all this? –*Metric_Martyr*

Downturn Abbey

Eye TV is proud to present the classic drama that the whole nation is talking about

The story so far... Agreeable, patrician aristocrat Lord Cameron is grooming the gauche, middle-class Nicholas Clegg in the traditional ways of the governing classes. Meanwhile, Lord Cameron's mysterious valet, Mr Coulson, seems to have a secret past. Events come to a head with the arrival of the telephone at Downturn Abbey...

⸺ EPISODE 95 ⸺

(The Library. Lord Cameron is reading a neatly ironed copy of the Daily Telegraph bearing headline: 'Yes, it's Lord Fellowes at last'. Lord Cameron smiles, but his mood darkens as his valet Coulson enters)

Coulson: You wanted to see me, sir.

Lord Cameron: Now, look here, Coulson, I've been given evidence that you're a bit of a bounder and should be in prison.

Coulson: I'd rather not talk about it, sir, for personal reasons.

Lord Cameron: Well, that's alright then. I shan't sack you after all. I shall instruct Mr Cable, the Butler, to stop making a fuss about nothing.

(Cut to the family eating lavish dinner)

Nicholas Clegg *(trying to eat soup with his fish knife)*: It has always been my opinion, my Lord, that the lower classes would benefit from free education.

Dame Maggie: Free education? I don't think so, Mr Clegg. If you allow them education then the lower classes will no longer be stupid enough to vote for you!

(There is an awkward silence. Only Lady George sniggers behind her fan)

Lady George: But Mr Clegg, may I be so bold as to enquire who is going to pay for all the oiks' free education?

Nicholas Clegg *(looks embarrassed and pours gravy into his wine glass)*: I... er... er...

(As ever, the gracious and noble Lord

Cameron intervenes)

Lord Cameron: Whilst we all admire your philanthropic motives, Nicholas, and they are greatly to your credit, Lady George does have a point. There is, I believe, a popular expression "There is no such thing as a free lunch".

Dame Maggie: What is "lunch"? I have heard of "luncheon" and indeed "bruncheon", but no one at Downturn has ever used the word "free".

Lord Cameron: What Dame Maggie is trying to say, Nicholas, is that there is a price to be paid for everything, including, I fear, education.

Nicholas Clegg: You're quite right, your Lordship. I have now completely changed my mind.

(At this point, the resentful footman, Hughes, deliberately empties the salt cellar over Nicholas Clegg's sherry trifle)

Dame Maggie: Oh dear, it would appear that we must take everything Mr Clegg says with a pinch of salt!

(Cut to the hallway, where the new telephone rings. Coulson shiftily picks it up and listens in)

To be continued...

"Sorry, kids, we've had to introduce parenting fees"

"Is that all you're selling... boots?"

Honours In Full

Lord Downton of Abbey (for services to the snobbery industry)

Dame Bakewell of Tart (for services to the crumpet industry)

Lord Gulam of Naan (for services to the currying favour industry)

Lord Greed of Grade (for services to the Ant & Dec industry)

Lord Fundraiser of Tory (for services to the Cameron industry)

Dame Shackleton of That Divorce (for services to the unshackling industry)

Lord Hedge of Fund (for financial services to himself)

(That's enough peers. Ed.)

HOW THE LIB DEMS ARE AFFECTING COALITION POLICY

OLD POLICY
Control Orders
Tuition fees
Obeying Cameron

NEW POLICY
Orders of control
Fees for tuition
Doing whatever Dave says

The Alternative Rocky Horror Service Book

No. 94 A Service to Celebrate the 400th Anniversary of the King James Authorised Version of the Holy Bible.

The President: Brethren and sisters, we are gathered here today to give thanks for one of the great works of world literature. We start with a reading from that wonderful book, *In Our Time* by Melvyn of Bragg.

Reader: **The King James Bible is one of the outstanding achievements of the English language, comparable to the works of Chaucer, Shakespeare and indeed myself. No book has had greater influence on the shaping of our culture, permeating every nook and cranny of our lives, from phrases used in everyday speech to the grand** cadences of our finest writers, such as Milton, Wordsworth and myself.

This is the word of the Lord Bragg.

All: Thanks be to Melve.

Hymn

"There is a Good Book far away
It's very old and boring
And if we read it in the church
You soon would all be snoring"

Prayer

The President: We give thanks today for the King James Bible, and for all those men and women who worked so hard behind the scenes, often for very little reward, to bring it to fruition. Let us pray that their efforts will not be forgotten, in this the 400th year since this great and indispensable work of literature first came to birth.

We further give thanks that we no longer have to use this book since much of the language is absurdly archaic and inaccessible, particularly to the young people who are more familiar with_____ (*at this point he may say "Twitter" or "Facebook", or some similar medium of modern communication*).

All: Wicked, cool, innit (*or possibly they may say "What on earth are you talking about?"*).

Dismissal

The President: The King James Version may have been all very well in its day, but I think we can do a lot better nowadays.

Closing Hymn

"Book of ages, not for me
Let's all go and have some tea"

(*The congregation shall then process to the Coffee Area where they shall be provided with coffee, tea or some similar beverage*)

© The Society for the Propagation of the Sid James Bible (Is this *right? Ed.*)

"I'm demonstrating against the appalling cuts I voted for"

NOT IN MY NAME

RSJ

DRAWING ALL FAITHS TOGETHER

Hi!
And I'm really looking forward to my next assignment, flying to Orlando, Florida, to address F.L.U.S.H., The Federation of Lavatorial Utilities and Sanitary Hygiene. But what, I hear you ask, is this to do with the mission of D.A.F.T., which is to unite people of different faiths?

Hey, it's easy, surely, to join up the dots! The simple daily act of going to the toilet is something which brings all faiths together, be we Christian, Jew, Hindu, Mohammedan, Buddhist, Scientologist or Jedi Knight.

And let's not forget that there are many people in the world who have not had the benefit of toilet paper, let alone a porcelain bowl and a chain to pull. It is their plight that drives me to Florida, to the HQ of F.L.U.S.H., to spread the message and pick up a cheque for £50,000 to help some of the world's needier women.

As I shall tell my audience of F.L.U.S.H. executives in the Ronald Reagan Suite of the Conrad Black Hilton, "We are all brothers and sisters on the toilet".

Yours,

Rev. T. Blair

Chief Executive, D.A.F.T. (former vicar of St. Albion's)

TOP ANGLICANS DEFECT OVER WOMEN BISHOPS

We've got to show who wears the trousers

"Quattro stagioni... Capricciosa... Giovanni Battista... What on earth is a Giovanni Battista?"

RBG

Royal Bank of Gnome

I APPLAUD Mr Cable's decision *not* to publish the Financial Services Authority's report into the collapse of the Bank of Gnome, of which I was Chairman, and the bank's rescue by the taxpayer to the tune of £94 billion.

Ignorant laymen have demanded that the *public* should be entitled to see the details of this complex investigation, but few of them would understand the intricacies of the international banking system, which led to the unfortunate purchase of the Dutch van Der Bummer Bank.

In retrospect, we can all see that this was probably the worst mistake in banking history and may well have precipitated the collapse of the entire western economy.

But no blame can conceivably attach to those responsible who acted in good faith and were deservedly awarded modest bonuses, totalling £95 billion for their efforts.

The FSA report *must* therefore remain confidential, as otherwise the general public might easily come to the conclusion that I and my colleagues were in some way a bunch of terrific crooks trying to steal their money – a suggestion as libellous as it is true.

Thank goodness that Mr Cable is capable of grasping this important principle in between dancing about on television.

Sir Fred Gnome,
Shred House,
Canary Wharf.

DAVID MILIBAND'S SHOCK NEW JOB

by Our Political Staff ANDREW MARRS BAR

THE world of Westminster was rocked to its foundations last night when it was announced that the former Foreign Secretary and aspirant for the Labour Party leadership, David Miliband, is to take an unexpected new job.

Rumours have been flying around the tea-rooms and bars of the Houses of Parliament that Mr Miliband was planning a startling new career, as possibly a teacher, a TV personality or even a Sunderland footballer.

Instead Mr Miliband has come up with something even more surprising.

Said his spokesman, "David has decided, after much thought and heart-searching, that he is going to dedicate himself to doing the job he is paid for by the taxpayers – ie representing his South Shields constituents as their MP."

"David knows," the spokesperson went on, "that this courageous decision will attract a lot of criticism, not least from his fellow MPs, who consider that he would be wasting his talents and that the only point of being an MP is to use it to get well-paid positions outside politics."

David Miliband is older than his brother, Ed.

GOVERNMENT 'HAD NO CHOICE' OVER BANKERS' BONUSES

by Our Banking Staff **Phil Boots**

A SPOKESMAN for the Government says it had no choice but to cave in over banks' bonus payments after threats that senior bankers would relocate from Britain overseas and destroy those economies instead.

"We must keep the very best banking talent here in London destroying our economy," insisted the spokesman. "The Square Mile must retain its status as a major player in the meltdown of our economy.

"If the banks were to withhold these bonuses, these City high-fliers would just take their skills for destroying economies elsewhere and surely none of us wants that."

Same Old Tory

Meanwhile, the Prime Minister David Cameron has praised the City for its restraint. He told reporters, "Hats off to those bankers who, after receiving their million pound bonuses, showed great restraint by then not waving the cash in Vince Cable's face nor mooning him whilst shouting 'loadsamoney, what you going to do about it twinkle toes?'".

Fib Dems

Mr Cable, however, came under criticism from his Lib Dem colleagues who accused him of doing a U-turn, having promised them that there would be a veto over bonuses. He denied this, telling them "There *is* a veto over bonuses. David Cameron is allowed to veto anything I say."

He continued, "I am delighted to confirm that, despite everything, I have forced a number of concessions from the banks. From now on, banks will have to limit paying the bonuses to bankers who actually work for them and they must show restraint when deciding on the level of bonuses, unless they don't want to." He concluded, "Er... that's it".

"We're still not lending"

PRESCOTT TAKES THE MONEY AND TRIES TO RUN – BUT TOO FAT

by Our Advertising Correspondent **Des Pratt**

LORD Prescott has rejected claims he's impugning the good name of MoneySupermarket.com by agreeing to appear this week in the House of Lords.

"The House of Lords is just a bit of knockabout fun, they offered me a lot of money to show up, so I didn't see any harm in it" insisted the retired pugilist.

"Most people can see my appearances were light hearted and strictly tongue in cheek."

"I take my obligations along-side Nigel Mansell and that bald

bloke towards upholding the good name of moneysupermarket.com very seriously indeed."

Neasden Central Police Station

The Personal Record of Detective Sergeant Kennington, Codename Beardie of the Yard

13 OCTOBER

0905 hrs Appointment with tattooist at Studs 'R' Us, 279 Pricerite Road, Neasden to arrange tattoo on arm bearing inscription, "I am not a copper". Cost £379.32p to come from secret account at NatWest in the name of "Mr Undercover Beardie".

1030 hrs Purchase false beard and dark glasses at Party Party, the novelty costume outfitters in Neasden High Street.

1200 hrs Attend meeting of subversive group, The Tufnell Park Eco-Spartists Against Nuclear Wind Farms (Chair: Ms Autumn Sunflower Fotherington-Thomas). Suggest armed, peaceful invasion of Battersea Power Station in protest at climate change. A vote is taken. For: 1 (myself). Against: 7 (everyone else).

1430 hrs Visit cashpoint and withdraw £2,000 expenses. Take delivery of 4x4 vehicle for touring European hot-spots in coming months.

1930 hrs Top secret assignation with Ms Autumn Sunflower Fotherington-Thomas to formulate strategy to bring M25 to a standstill as protest against Boris Bikes. Propose motion that discussions continue on a horizontal basis. Carried unanimously.

2000 hrs To allay suspicions that I am undercover policeman I beat myself up on Save The Tuna Rally and make front page of Guardian. Receive congratulatory message from my handler Secret Inspector Knacker at Covert Ops HQ – codenamed "Scotland Yard". I am informed that my intelligence ie, that many young people do not approve of Nuclear Power, has been fast-tracked and placed on the desk of Tony Blair no less.

2400 hrs I arrest myself for having "gone native". Fellow members of the Dollis Hill Friends of The Badger Revolutionary Alliance are shocked – as all seven of them have also been working undercover as agents provocateurs.

0100 hrs Take plane to begin new life in New Neasden, Ohio, using codename "Operation Waste of Public Money".

For a fuller version of Sgt Kennington's log go to the website agentprovocateur@lingerieerotique.com

DESPERATE BUSINESS

JON & MICK / MODERN TOSS

Alright, I'm thinking of watching the London marathon on telly, do you want to sponsor me?

I see you're interested in going on a skills re-training course, what areas did you have in mind?

not fussed mate, anything to get me out of the office

how's it going?

not bad, I've been boosting my wages with a bit of medical trials work

I'm thinking about taking early retirement

how early?

about 2.30

THE RIDDLE OF THE SPHINX

If Mubarak is such a bastard, why did the West support him for thirty years?

Er...

What next for Egypt?

JUBILANT scenes in square... moment of history... reverberations throughout Middle East... Berlin Wall... voice of the Arab street... bloodless revolution... shockwaves felt by neighbouring dictatorships... domino effect... note of caution... need for orderly transition... stability paramount... army good thing... or not... to be honest we haven't a clue... Foreign Office useless... newspapers even worse... er... er.

© All newspapers

Daily Cairograph

Friday, 4th February, 2011

Hated Dictator Clings to Power – But For How Long?

BY OUR MAN IN WAPPING **A. HAQ**

Autocrat Murdarok with his feared flame-haired enforcer Rebekah Wadi known as "The Terror of the Paedos"

S HIS empire crumbles around his ears the 80-year-old dictator Ruhpah Murdarok, who for over thirty years has ruled with an iron rod, is staring into the abyss.

As even his loyal lieutenants begin to fall out, the man they call "Al Diggah" is facing a popular uprising, with thousands of celebrities now insisting that his regime of secret surveillance and intimidation must end.

Murdarok tried to appease his critics by suggesting a handover of power to his equally hated son James but to no avail.

In de Nile

Said one celebrity, "All we want is for Murdarok to go and take his ghastly family with him."

Murdarok is believed to have amassed an enormous fortune, much of it deposited in American banks. If he chose to flee he would still have many friends in America.

International opinion, however, is hardening against him. Even former friends such as UK Prime Minister, David Cameron, are now calling for "an orderly handover of power" to prevent chaos and anarchy engulfing Wapping.

Said one observer, "It is beginning to look like Murdarok's days of exploiting ordinary people for personal gain are finally numbered and *(cont. p.94)*

Nursery Times

Friday, January 21, 2011

OLD MOTHER GOOSE WINS DISCRIMINATION CASE

by Our Legal Staff **Sue Everyone**

IN A landmark case that has sent shock-waves throughout Nurseryland the veteran presenter Old Mother Goose has won her action against the Bedtime Broadcasting Corporation.

Old Mother Goose claimed that she was sacked from her job on a programme about country matters because "she was old and a mother".

Life of O'Reilly

In her evidence to the court Old Mother Goose (95) said, "I was replaced by Little Bo Peep solely on the grounds that she is young and pretty. I know a great deal more about country matters than Ms Peep, who cannot even look after sheep without losing them".

She went on to describe Ms Peep as "a flibbertigibbet air-headed bonneted bimbo!".

Rumpolestiltskin of the Bailey

Speaking for the BBC, Ms Jay Huntryfile (31) denied the accusation of "institutional ageism" pointing to the fact that Old Macdonald (98) was kept on as an expert on farming matters despite the fact that he was even older than Old Mother Goose.

Ms Huntryfile denied all charges of ageism saying "Old Mother Goose has clearly lost the plot, probably because she is so old".

Radio Four Score and Ten

The result of the case was welcomed as a triumph for older women. Said Old Mother Goose, "If I had not bravely brought this case to a successful conclusion, none of Nurseryland's veteran broadcasting stars would have been safe. Not Old Mother Hubbard, not Old Mother Niddety Nod, not even Anne Robinson".

ON OTHER PAGES

● *The Cheshire Fat Cat – Why is he grinning all the way to the bank?* **3**

● *"I Was Right to Shop Wee Willie Winkie to Police" says Mrs Winkie* **4**

● *Gingerbread House Prices To Fall by 10%* **94**

"They've all heard your MRI scan story before, Gerald"

The Film They're All Talking About

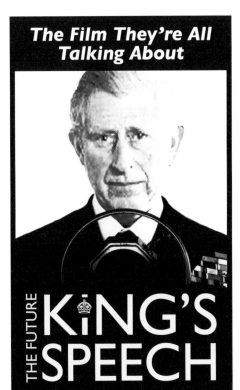

THE FUTURE KING'S SPEECH

THE HEARTWARMING royal story of the shy, diffident old man who suddenly has to take on the burden of the throne of England, when he has only been waiting for it for over 60 years.

Poor Charles has an appalling problem with his speech. Every time he opens his mouth, all that comes out is an embarrassing stream of nonsense.

We see him desperately struggling to say something interesting and important that will unite the nation in "the great war to preserve, you know, this global harmony thingie, that we all, in a very real sense, hope to, you know... polar bears... Indian version of Poundbury... Chelsea Barracks... defender of the interfaith... it really is, what's the word, appalling."

If only he could manage to say the words that would make him truly popular – "I am handing over the throne to William". But would it ever happen?

Cast in full

King Charles III..............Colin Firth
Queen Camilla.......................................
Helena Bonham-Carter
1st Corgi........................Timothy Spall

Don't miss the film that is already being tipped to win every Oscar in every category at this year's Academy Awards

---

Letters to the Editor

The King's Speech

SIR – Much as I enjoyed the recent film "The King's Speech" I could not help wondering why the screenwriters felt obliged to tamper with well known historical facts.

For example the scene where the Duke of Windsor is shown speaking with a German accent to his valet bears no relation to the truth. And for George Vth to be depicted sticking a set of Zimbabwean stamps into his album in 1936 when Zimbabwe was, as we all know, then still the Protectorate of British Rumbabaland is quite ludicrous. And the film is not merely littered with historical inaccuracies. At one point our future queen looks out of the window at Buckingham Palace and there are snowdrops on the lawn – when it is quite clearly August Bank Holiday!

As for the supposed stammer of King George VI, my uncle Admiral Sir Alan Chrichton-Gussett met him on a number of occasions in the course of his duties as Knight Commander of the Royal Bedchamber and told me, in the strictest confidence, that the King spoke fluently in several languages and the difficulty was never to get him to speak but to shut him up!

Sir Herbert Gussett
The Old Stuttery,
Stutford-on-Avon, Stuts.

That Camilla/Kate advisory lunch menu

Spring Chicken and Game Old Bird

Smoky Trout and Fresh sKate

New Lamb and Grilled Mutton

– ✳ –

Future Queen of Puddings
(expect a wait of at least 25 years)

– ✳ –

To drink:
Bubbly Brunette and Vintage Blonde
(That's enough menu, Ed)

THAT ADVICE IN FULL

1 Watch out for predatory older women with designs on your husband
2 Er...
3 That's it

'NO SPECIAL TREATMENT FOR MURDOCH,' Says Culture Secretary Hunt

by Our Political Staff **Monopolly Toynbee**

CULTURE supremo Jeremy Hunt today explained why he was giving Sky Mogul Rupert Murdoch "as much time as he needs" to come up with a good reason why Murdoch should be allowed to control all the media in Britain.

"Mr Murdoch," said Mr Hunt, "is a very old man and it takes him much longer to think up reasons why we should do whatever he says."

Stupid Hunt

"There is no favouritism here," the minister for Culture, Murdoch and Sport commented in an exclusive interview with Sky TV in conjunction with the Times, the Sun and the News of the World. "It's just that

we're terrified of him."

At a recent top-level private dinner with the prime minister, Mr Murdoch hinted that there could be a downside to any refusal to sanction his bid.

He told the Prime Minister, "You fuck with me, you pommie posh boy, and you and that pooftah friend of yours, Clegg, are toast."

Mr Murdoch is 106.

STOP PRESS

Sky supremo Rupert Murdoch has offered to set up a high-level board to guarantee "the complete editorial independence" of all Sky output, particularly Sky News.

The members of the board will include Mr Rupert Murdoch, Mr James Murdoch, Ms Elizabeth Murdoch and the distinguished sports commentator Mr Andy Gray.

"Can you get that? I'm putting the kids to bed"

Chilcot Enquiry Day 94 **Blair Recalled**

Sir John Chilcot: It is very kind of you to come, Mr Blair, and very good of you to give up some of your valuable time to answer a few questions – we do realise you have a pressing engagement later today, addressing a luncheon meeting of the Kazakhstan Institute of Toxic Waste at the Dorchester Hotel.

Blair: I'm doing what I think is right. Obviously, others may take a different view, but they are wrong.

Sir Roderic Hard-Lyne: Mr Blair, it has been suggested that you put pressure on the Attorney General to change his mind about the legality of the Iraq War. When you first gave evidence, you said this was untrue. Have you changed your mind at all on this?

Blair: No, I've looked through my files to check this and I stick to my original account, which is that an Angel of the Lord appeared unto Mr Goldsmith by night, saying to him, "You must change your mind". And Mr Goldsmith woke and did the right thing.

Chilcot: Well, that certainly clears that up. Thank you very much indeed.

Baroness Uttar Rubesh: One further question, Mr Blair. Will you sign this copy of your book? It's not for me, it's for my nephew.

Blair: Certainly. That will be ten pounds, please.

(To be continued...)

TITANIC: CHANGING COURSE NOW 'WOULD BE A MISTAKE'

by Our Drowning Street Correspondent **P. Fortey-Five**

CAPTAIN Osborne has announced that he has no intention of changing course, in spite of the severe iceberg warnings he has just received giving him notice of an imminent collision.

"I have no intention of moving from our appointed path", he said over the noise of the rats (surely 'bankers'?) swiftly launching the boats.

To a chorus of "We're all going to die", he added, "we are maintaining course, and things can only get better. A scenario where all the third class passengers are left to drown as the rich abandon ship is absolutely absurd".

The Alternative Rocky Horror Service Book

No. 94 A Service of Watery Welcome (formerly Holy Baptism).

The President: Hello everyone.

All: Hi.

The President: I'd first of all like to say welcome to the parents *(here he may say Sandra and Philip or Colin and Nigel or Trish and Maggie).*

All: Awesome.

The President: And not forgetting the star of the show *(here he indicates the infant).* What name have you chosen, guys? *(Here the parents may give the name or names they have selected: Starburst or Hosni or Peregrine Worsthorne).* Will the "Baby buddies", what we used to

call Godparents, please step forward?

The Solemn Vows

The President: Do you, Baby buddy, promise to take an interest in the general wellbeing of our little friend here?

Baby buddy: Cool.

The President: And do you, Baby buddy, further pledge to remember to give a Top Shop voucher or iTunes card to baby N or M at Christmas and birthdays?

Baby buddy: We shall remember them. *(At this point there will be a reading from an interview with St Elton John the Baptist or some similar uplifting commentary on the nature of positive parenthood.)*

The Watery Welcome

*(Here the President will take the baby N or M, having first satisfied the Criminal Records Bureau that he or she is a fit and proper person to make physical contact with a minor. The President will then place the baby, in the Church paddling pool with some suitable toys – it may be a rubber duck or a sustainable fish, but **not** a submarine.)*

The President: You may now take pictures of the baby but only those of you who have undergone a full vetting process from the social services.

All: Whatever.

The President: Will we now sing Hymn 94, "By the Rivers of Babylon" by Boney M, and the parents have just asked me to say that you will all be welcome back at their place for a big booze-up as soon as this boring bit is over.

All: Way to go!

Approved by the General Synod of the Church of England, 2011

GLENDA SLAGG

The Best Lines-Woman in Fleet Street (Geddit ?!?!!)

■ FOR crying out loud!?!! What's gone wrong with us Brits??!!! Can't we take a joke any more??! So two boorish blokes on the telly like to have a bit of banter about us gorgeous gals!!!!? And now they've lost their jobs for Gawd's sake!! Talk about a humour by-pass!!? Have we gone stark staring mad???! Come on Sky TV, give Andy Gray 'n' Robert Keys their jobs back??! So they can continue to make us laugh a leering' and a jeerin' at the touchline totty!!?! *(is this right? Ed)*

■ ANDY Gray and Robert Keys – what a disgrace!!??! Talk about sexist pigs – these oinkers take the bacon!!! And DON'T tell us gals that it's all a joke and we haven't got a sense of humour!?! 'Cos we have – and we're laughing at you!!! But some things are beyond a joke and

theses mindless, mouthy, morons have set the cause of women right back to the Stone Age!?!! Ug ug ug!! That's caveman speak for "Get lost and Good Riddance"!?!! Geddit?!?!

Byeeeeeee

SKY SPORT SEXISM SHOCK

It's a game of two half-wits

BBC Radio 3

Opera Highlights

Berlusconi's Cosi Fan Prostitutti

Act 94

THE Robber Baron is besieged by a chorus of dancing girls, courtesans and female members of the European Parliament, angrily accusing him of seducing their virtue in return for large sacks of gold.

A trio of the fallen women, Signorinas Bunga Bunga, Rumpi Pumpi and Lotta Totti, sing the haunting aria *Mille e tre* ("How on earth could he have sex with 1,003 of us in one night?").

There is a clap of thunder and Pope Benedict appears on a throne above the stage. He issues an anathema

on the Robber Baron, warning him that he will be dragged down to hell and eternal damnation unless he repents and changes his ways. His Holiness sings the dramatic baritone solo *Basta Silvio!* ("See Nipples and Die").

But the Baron is unafraid and laughs him to scorn. He sings *Just one Pornetto*, and rings up for yet another agreeable 22-year-old companion to be delivered to the Palazzo Fornicazzione this time dressed as a nurse in order to reflect Silvo's concern for the state of Italy's health services.

The Holy Father retreats in confusion, as the stage fills with a chorus of adoring male voters, all pledging undying support for Silvio as they sing *Donna Kebab* ("Give her one for us, Silvio").

The curtain falls, but not on the Government.

"It's a bungabungalow"

ITALIAN SEX PARTIES HERE

WHAT YOU WON'T READ IN THE SUN

NEWS IN BRIEFS

Lovely Rebekah welcomes the sacking of Andy Gray and Robert Keys and hopes that this will see an end to institutional sexism of the type that is rife in newspapers run by herself.

"Nigel and I have decided to try for a divorce"

That Honorary Degree Citation In Full

SALUTAMUS GILBERTUS ET GEORGOS DUO ARTIFICES BRITTANES LABORENT IN OSTUM ENDI LONDINI SUNT CELEBRISSIMI PER MULTI FACTI ARTI PULCHRISSIMUM PER EXEMPLA 'GEORGOS PUDENDUM ET GILBERTUS TURDA' ET 'LABIA SCUMMA' ET 'IN TURDI' ET 'CRUENTUS LUNA' ET 'EXCREMENTABILE NUDI MUNDI HUMANUS' ET 'NUDI IMAGI EXCREMENTI' ET 'EJACULUM SANGUINUM URINUM FAECUM SPUTUM' ET CETERA ET CETERA AD NAUSEAM ANNO MMVIII SUNT SUBIUNCTI IN MATRIMONIO GILBERTUS ET GEORGUS DICAT UT MARGARETA THATCHERI ET PRINCEPS CAROLUM ADMIRATI SUNT SED FORTASSE THATCHERI NON REDDET LAUDIS NON EST IMPORTANTUS PER DUO SUNT CELEBRISSIMI ET HABENT DIVES MASSIVI SED TRISTIS EST UT IMPERATOR NON HABET VESTI

© Universitatum Ostum Londinium MMX

Dave Snooty AND HIS PALS

'Radio 4 Audience Must Move North,' BBC Is Told

by Our Media Staff **Sal Ford** and **Di Versity**

A SHOCK report on the BBC's radio output has revealed the astonishing fact that the majority of listeners to Radio 4 are white, middle-class, live in the South of England, are keen on gardening and like listening to The Archers.

Says the report's author, top TV executive David Liddlebrain, "It's a national scandal to which there can only be one remedy – the entire Radio 4 audience must be forced to relocate to the North of England, paid for by the BBC at a modest cost of £5 trillion."

Shock

"Of course," Mr Liddlethought continued, "there will be protests from the usual Disgusted-of-Tunbridge Wells Brigade, saying that they don't want to move to Manchester, but they must be ignored in the cause of building a diversity template that reflects our national audience demographic."

Asked what he meant by this sentence, Mr Liddleidea replied,

after consulting his iPad, "I've no idea. I'll have to get back to you after lunch".

Other sections of the report call for a major shake-up of other parts of the BBC network which are perceived to be "over-serving a particular audience sector".

For instance, the report blasts the BBC's Radio 1 for being obsessed with young people and concentrating on pop music which "does not appeal to the majority of white, middle-class listeners who live in the south of England".

Particular criticism was levelled at the BBC's Asian Network for appealing only to Asian listeners living in Britain.

"It is time this cultural ghetto was opened up to a much wider audience," the report stated, "such as Afro-Caribbean women, the Inuit community, Scientologists and members of the white middle-class living in the South of England who are keen on gardening and listening to The Archers."

Radio 4: THE ARCHERSICKOFTHEM

So, what's it like being in a long-running soap?

I liked it when Diana got written out

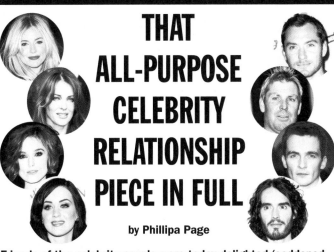

THAT ALL-PURPOSE CELEBRITY RELATIONSHIP PIECE IN FULL

by Phillipa Page

Friends of the celebrity couple were today delighted/saddened to hear that Sienna/Liz/Kiera/Katy and Jude/Shane/Rupert/Russell had split up/got back together again.

Said a spokesman for the couple, "Obviously they are very happy/devastated that the relationship has hit the rocks/been reignited and would greatly appreciate it if the press would allow them some privacy/give them a lot more publicity."

"Oh, right… thanks. So how do you attach it to the computer?"

QUESTION TIME

Dimbleby "Ok, we've got time for one last question – the lady at the back there, yes you."

Anna Ford "Thank you. I was wondering what the panel thinks about the fact that aging men continue to secure lucrative deals with

the BBC when equally talented women fail to even… (interrupted)".

Dimbleby "Yes, well sadly we appear to have run out of time, many thanks to tonight's panel – goodnight".

Silly twiddly music plays out over credits

The Seven Ages of Man

EXCLUSIVE TO ALL PAPERS
Libya: An Apology

IN RECENT weeks and months and years we may have railed against Western military action in the Middle East, saying that the misguided decision to send military forces into oil rich countries like Iraq on the premise of removing a brutal dictator from power was sheer folly, as all that resulted were tensions in the region being further inflamed.

We now realise, in the light of Col Gaddafi's brutal suppression of the rebels in Libya, that nothing could be further from the truth, and that the West cannot stand by impotently and allow Gaddafi to remain in power when swift and targeted military intervention in the region, with the laudable aim of removing a brutal dictator from power, would undoubtedly calm inflamed tensions in the region.

We apologise for any confusion caused and any confusion in the future when the West (cont. p. 94).

DUNKIRK TIMES

Friday, March 4, 2011

'Our Finest Hour' – Historic Evacuation A Triumph For Britain

BY BEN GHAZI AND LIBBY YAH

TODAY, as thousands of stranded Britons stood on the beaches of Tripoli, waiting to be rescued from the armed might of an evil dictator, I witnessed a miracle of heroism and pluck.

Britain had not deserted them in their hour of need.

The Foreign Secretary Sir Winston Hague pledged that he would do everything in his power to bring them home by Christmas (subject to availability of Easyjet aircraft).

Field Marshal Hague

Less than 48 hours after the SOS went out from the vast crowd of heroic businessmen trapped on the sands of the Libyan coast, a lone aircraft still stood on the runway at Gatwick, waiting for somebody to mend a fuse. Meanwhile, the Royal Navy had once again risen to the challenge.

A fleet of one little ship, HMS Cucumber, set sail from the scrapyard, where it was about to be broken up under the latest round of defence cuts, and is now only waiting for permission from Col. Gaddafi before it embarks on its vital task of rescuing the stranded and desperate British oil executives.

Notes & queries

What is this 'mojo' which Foreign Secretary William Hague claims not to have lost?

(Selwyn Ringbinder, Worcester)

Rev. Catflap is entirely wrong when she says that "Mojo" is a Zen Buddhist term meaning "inner peace and quietude" set out in the 9th century Tibetan Book of the Yak. What nonsense! "Mojo" derives from the famous American basketball player Moses Johnson (no relation to Boris, I hasten to add) who played for the Cincinnati Slamdunks between 1952 and 1954. Johnson, who was 7ft 2ins, was famous for his post-hoop celebratory dance known as the "Mojo".
Mrs Covonia D'Anconia, Sidcup

I am sorry to correct your correspondent Mrs D'Anconia but her baseball story is pure hokum. The "Mojo" is an invigorating alcoholic cocktail consisting of equal parts of vermouth, gin, brandy, lemonade, methylated spirits and unleaded gasoline. It was popular in Las Vegas during the Great Depression and was named after the tribe of American Indians, the Mojo, who lived in the nearby Nevada desert. Mr Hague could perhaps benefit from one of these beverages before he makes anymore foreign affairs decisions!
Colonel Jim Guantanamo (Rtd), Oregon

Answers to the following please:

Who invented the Bendy bus? Can ostriches swim? What is Peter McKay's real name?

'NO FRY ZONE' DEMANDED

THERE have been increasing calls all around the world for the immediate implementation of a No-Fry Zone above the United Kingdom. If imposed it would effectively prevent Stephen Fry banging on about how marvellously calming taking cocaine is, particularly when you are trying to do the Times crossword. However critics point out that it would be almost impossible to achieve a No-Fry Zone as he has complete control of the airwaves and the blogosphere and his millions of fanatical followers make such a measure virtually unachievable.

■ Full story p. 94

The Eye's Controversial New Columnist

This week, I am very angry about the so-called "media" criticising William Hague. This makes me very angry indeed. Leave him alone, I say! I may know absolutely nothing about nothing, as I am a baby *(see photo)*, but I do know what it's like to be bald and helpless, unable to communicate the simplest things and always being on the verge of tears. If you could all crawl in our booties for half an hour, then you'd certainly understand why we both get a bit *(cont. p. 94)*

"I do wish you wouldn't stop and let complete strangers use the loo"

41

ROYAL WEDDING
That Shock Guest List in Full

The King of Bahrain (Subject to availability)

Sir David Beckham and Lady Victoria Posh

Charlie Ricketson-Smythe and Arabella Anstruther-Starborgling

His Royal Highness Prince Harry Windsor and Ms Chelsea Town-Hall (Subject to availability)

His Royal Highness Prince Andrew and Miss Lollita Masseuse, 17

Sir Elton and Lady John

Baby Zachariah John

The Grand Duke Vladimir of All the Russias

Guy 'Tosser' Tossington-Ffolkes and the Hon. Pandora Cholmondley-Jones

The Emir of Gasakstan

Air Vice-Marshal Sir Horace Norris and Lady Horatia Norris

Mr R.J. Kipling, headmaster of St. Cake's School

Captain Daws-Toumanual and Mrs Dolly Trolly, representing Easyjet

Mr William Clinton, representing the President of the United States

Mrs Jilly Hockey-Stix, former Matron St Crumpets Preparatory School

Mr and Mrs Asda Patel, proprietors Jet Services convenience store, Fast Bucklebury

Sir William Shawcross, Biographer Royal by Appointment to the late Queen Mother

Fight Lieutenant 'Pongo' Squiffy-Squiffington, Air Sea Rescue

Sir Stephen Fry

His Holiness the Dalai Lama

Taki Takalotofcokupthenos (Restricted view)

ˈPhil and Sandra Snell, proprietors the Dog and Duck, Stanford Dingley

Ms Tara Rara-Boomdeeay (to bring wedding coke – *surely 'cake'? Ed*)

Mr Colin Firth, representing the late King George VI

For a full list of wedding guests go to: www.madeuplist/sadtelegraph.co.uk

HEALTH WARNINGS ARE BAD FOR YOU
Shock New Health Warning

by Our Scare Staff **Phil PaperonMondaybecausethere'snotmuchnews**

YES. It's official. Health warnings are bad for you. A new survey by the Department of Health Warnings has found conclusive evidence that health warnings about eating meat, drinking wine, using mobile phones, taking aspirin, going to the gym, breathing, living and reading the Daily Mail are guaranteed to make you ill and shorten your life by "up to ten years".

This follows on from the report yesterday which claimed that health warnings were *good* for you. This was based on a survey by the Department of Health Warnings which found conclusive evidence that health warnings about eating meat, drinking wine, using mobile phones, taking aspirin, going to the gym, breathing, living and reading the Daily Mail are guaranteed to make you *well* and extend your life expectancy by "up to ten years".

Said a spokesperson for the Department of Health Warnings, "These two surveys are in no way contradictory. Both are rubbish and you would do much better to have a nice steak and a glass of red wine with an aspirin whilst phoning a friend on your mobile to arrange to meet in the gym *(That's enough space-filling on a Monday when there is no news, Ed.)*

"I've got another 40 years to live!"

POLLY FILLER
on Tiger Mums

WE'VE all been reading recently about the Tiger Mums. They are the new breed of driven Chinese über-mums who make sure their kids end up as high-achieving A* students with a minimum Grade 8 piano and violin who would rather read Dostoevsky than watch America's Top Model or play on the Xbox!

They are tough. They are focused. They hold down top jobs whilst producing extraordinarily gifted, successful and disciplined children who love them for it. Ring any bells? Yes, because that's me all over. And I'm not even Chinese!

However, my au pair *is* and thanks to my no-nonsense, tough approach, Wok Maw brings up Charlie the Chinese way! No sitting around for him – unlike his useless father Simon who spends all day watching Extreme Strictly Come Extra Factor Dancing On Ice with Konnie Huq. You're too late, Saddo Simon, and btw she's married to Charlie Brooker who *doesn't* just sit around watching TV all day... oh, ok, yes he does... but... where was I?

No, Toddler Charlie is busy, busy, busy doing Further Maths, Advanced Mandarin, Nuclear Physics and perfecting Rach 3 for his end of term piano recital at The Hothouse Nursery – much better, incidentally, than his old school, St Tweedles For The Differently Gifted, which he had to leave after the unfortunate incident with the fire extinguisher. Anyway, the truth is I am not embarrassed about being a Tiger Mum. So what if I'm a pushy parent? Au pairs respond to being pushed hard and, at the end of the day, nothing gives me greater pleasure than hearing Wok Maw crying with happiness late at night in her room.

Sayonara!

Yours,

Pol Lee Fil Ah

This column appears in Polly Filler's hilarious new collection 'Chinese Bairns! A Guide To Bringing Up Your Children The Eastern Way' (Pearson, Johnson and Candy, £19.99)

Exclusive to Private Eye – that Census Form in Full

Official UK Census 2011

Sponsored by the Lockheed-Martin Arms Corporation – "Weapons we got 'em!"

IMPORTANT The data on this form is strictly confidential and the information contained therein will only be made available to the following organisations: ■ HM Government ■ HM Revenue and Customs ■ HM Police ■ Europol ■ News International ■ Anyone who pays up front.

WARNING Failure to complete the 918 boxes on this form will lead to an automatic £1,000 fixed penalty and/or detention without trial for 90 days in HMP Guantanamo Bay.

1. What is your full name?

2. What is it really?

3. What is your UK address?

4. Why is it different from the one you have given to the Department of Work and Pensions?

5. How many rooms are there in your house?

6. How many of them have you let out to Islamic terrorists/members of the travelling community/Members of Parliament claiming that your house is their primary residence?

7. How many toilets are there in your garden, and are they accessible to disabled members of the cottaging community?

8. How would you describe your gender?
a) male ☐ b) female ☐
c) pre-op transsexual ☐ d) reassigned hermaphrodite ☐ e) undecided ☐
f) Sir Peregrine Worsthorne ☐

9. Sexual orientation. Would you describe yourself as: a) heterosexual ☐
b) homosexual ☐ c) bi-sexual ☐

d) tri-sexual ☐   e) omnisexual ☐
f) would prefer a cup of tea and watching David Attenborough ☐

10. Religious orientation. Which of the following would best describe your belief system? a) Post-Christian Christianity ☐
b) Evangelical atheism ☐
c) Wicca/Paganism ☐   d) Scientology ☐
e) Worship of the Duke of Edinburgh ☐
f) Climate change denial ☐
g) Belief in the omnipresence and omniscience of Sir Stephen Fry ☐
h) Liberal reform moderate Jihadism ☐
i) Jedi Knightism ☐ *(Warning: anyone ticking this entry will be arrested for wasting the time of the census monitors and will be sentenced to 30 days community service on the planet Tatooine)*

11. Which is your favourite TV celebrity chef? Is it a) Heston Blumenthal ☐
b) Delia Smith ☐ c) The bald one from Masterchef ☐   d) Nigella Lawson ☐
e) Dominic Lawson ☐   f) Lord Lawson of Blubby? ☐

12. Which is your favourite Lockheed-Martin weapons system? Simply enter our Census Competition and you could win a nuclear-ground-air-to-air-missile of your choice. Just answer this simple question: Who is the President of the United States? Is it: a) President George W. Bush ☐ b) President John F. Kennedy ☐ c) L. Ron Hubbard ☐ d) Elvis Presley ☐

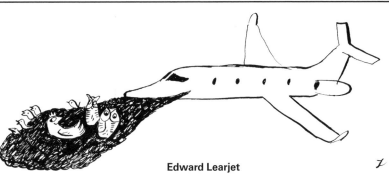

Edward Learjet

NEVER TOO OLD

by award-winning romantic novelist Dame Sylvie Krin,
author of *Heir of Sorrows* and *Duchess of Hearts*

THE STORY SO FAR: Media mogul Rupert Murdoch is celebrating his 80th birthday in his penthouse suite in Manhattan. Now read on...

"POP!" The champagne cork flew merrily from the bottle and Rupert gazed round at the group of assembled well-wishers who had gathered to honour him on this great occasion. And what a glittering cast of celebrities they were!

There was Sir David Frost resplendant in a wheelchair. "Hello, good evening and welcome," the great British broadcaster said to whoever would listen.

And there was Rebekah Brooks, the flame-haired first lady of News International, his great global company, shouting into her telephone!

And there was Glen Moron, Fox TV's legendary, political commentator, delighting Rupert's children with his jokes about President Obama being a Muslim terrorist!

There were some other people too, who Rupert did not quite recognise but he was sure that in all his long career, he had never seen such a dazzling assembly of VIPs.

But someone was missing. Who was it? the old man wondered, but try as he could, the name just would not come.

However, there was no time to worry about whether he was losing his grip, as suddenly the lights dimmed and a giant cake was wheeled forward by a team of white-coated chefs and the band struck up the familiar strains of "For he's a jolly old fellow!"

Rupert gazed in awe at the spectacle of the satellite dish-themed cake, but nervously wondered whether he would have sufficient puff to blow out all 80 candles.

However, before he could draw breath there was a mighty drum roll, a clash of cymbals, the cake exploded and out jumped the bikini-clad figure of his beautiful bride, the Queen of the Orient, Wendi Deng herself!

"Suplize! Suplize! Lupert," she cried, flinging her arms wide. "I hope you don't have big heart attack, glandad!"

(To be continued...)

Murdoch At 80

THERE is no denying that Rupert Murdoch is an incredible force of nature. Even critics describe him as a media visionary... print revolution... Wapping... BSkyB... Digital age... Fox TV... New York Times... Incredibly powerful... owns everything. Please don't sack me/can I have a job, please? *(cont. p. 94)*

SIR FRED'S SECRET

I screwed the entire country

"My, Granny – what a small pension you've got"

Daily Mail

FRIDAY, MARCH 18, 2011

TSUNAMI THREAT TO HOUSE PRICES – NOW IT'S SERIOUS

by Mail Staff **Sue Nami** and **Eartha Quake**

WE THOUGHT it was bad when Japan was destroyed and its nuclear reactors blew up but no one had prepared us for the shockwaves that reached the shores of Britain

As fears of a radioactive meltdown engulfing the entire planet grew, UK house prices looked set to tumble by an unprecedented 0.4%.

Said estate agent Jeremy Chancer, of respected property consultants Chancer, Wideboy and Krook, "If you are thinking of selling, now is a good time before the world ends.".

KEY

AND WHAT MAKES YOU FEEL YOU QUALIFY FOR INCAPACITY BENEFIT.

NEW ANDREW SHOCK
His Close Links To Infernal Despot

by Our Staff From Hell **B.L. Zebub and Lucy Fer**

THE beleaguered Duke of York faced new criticism over the revelation that he had several meetings with "one of the most unsavoury rulers in the universe".

Photographs show him relaxed and smiling, in initimate conversation with the man who has been described as "the most evil person there has ever been".

Known to the world only as "the Devil", the After-Life President of Satanistan is notorious for his long record of crimes against humanity.

Load of Bosch

A spokesman for Amnesty last night posted on Facebook pictures by the distinguished war artist Hieronymous Bosch, showing horrifying scenes of the Devil and his henchmen engaging in acts of torture, mass killings, mutilation, cannibalism and paedophilia.

Devil In Detail

"These pictures show beyond doubt," said the spokesman, "that it is entirely inappropriate for a member of the Royal Family to be associating with the leader of such an unacceptable regime."

10 Downing Street, however, was yesterday defending the Prince's role, saying that the Prime Minister has "complete confidence" in the Duke of York in his role of selling toasting forks, grid irons and carbon-neutral firelighters to our old ally, His Satanic Majesty.

The Satan Of Onan

But there was renewed disquiet over documents published by WickedLeaks, revealing a secret deal between Prince Andrew and the Devil,

in which the Devil agreed to purchase the Prince's "soul", in return for a life of jet-set luxury and perks of every kind.

The documents seem to show that this "unholy pact" gave the Prince unlimited access to private yachts, fast cars and meetings with under-age private masseuses.

However, buried in the small print of the contract is a so-called "Faustian Clause", under which the Prince, in the event of his death, would become subject for an indefinite period to various forms of eternal punishment.

It is thought that the Prince was unaware of the terms of this clause when he signed the agreement.

DEATH OF ANDREW'S CAREER: BLAIR GIVES EULOGY

He was the Paedo's Prince

DUM SNUBS DEE ON HIS BIG DAY

By our Political Staff **Lewis Carol Thatcher**

WHEN Tweedledum goes to the altar with his beautiful bride there will be one person conspicuously absent from his side – twin brother Tweedledee.

Relations between the two brothers are said to be at rock bottom since their much publicised fight over who should hold the coveted rattle.

When Tweedledum was victorious, Tweedledee retired from the front-line of nursery rhymes but has never forgiven his younger brother for stealing the prize rattle from under his nose.

Sources close to Dum told us, "Dee cannot be the Best Man since he has already been declared the Second Best Man".

Now Nursery Times readers can vote on who they would like to see at

Dum's right hand as he gets married and says "I do – whatever my spin doctor tells me".

YOU CHOOSE

❶ **Kinnochio**. Long nosed, long-winded Welsh-born puppet. Known to be one of Dum's few admirers.

❷ **The Mad Hattersley**. Elderly eccentric Tea Party Leader.

❸ **Mr Ed**. The talking Balls *(surely Horse? Ed)*

The Liz Taylor I Never Knew

By Everybody

I will never forget the time my editor said, "I want a thousand words on Liz Taylor by lunchtime".

How can I begin to describe my feelings about the legend that was Liz Taylor?

I first encountered the screen goddess on Wikipedia and I was immediately struck by her extraordinary career, which I copied and pasted into this piece.

But I was to come across Liz Taylor again. This time on the Internet Movie Database (IMDB) where I was impressed by her detailed filmography and fascinating information that her nickname was "Kitten", she was 5 foot 2 inches and her star sign was Pisces.

But the last time Liz Taylor

came into my life was shortly before my deadline when the clippings file arrived on my desk – late, of course, but then that was entirely befitting of the actress they called "A Luminous Beauty", "Hollywood's Last Goddess", "The Queen of the Screen", "A Charismatic Icon" and the "Brightest Star in the Film Firmament".

Yes, I will never forget the woman known simply as "My Features Editor" who told me in her warm, witty, wise and all too human way: "This is rubbish – I'll run it over 5 pages".

The question the whole nation is asking

KATE: IS THIS TOO THIN?

by Our Skeleton Staff **Liz Bones**

IT IS becoming more and more obvious to anyone who has cast an eye over the recent articles about the forthcoming royal wedding that the Kate Middleton coverage is quite alarmingly thin.

Of course it's quite normal for articles about weddings to be thin. There's not much to say and very little meat to go on.

But with Kate it is in a different league of thinness. The pieces are slender, emaciated, feeble, lifeless and lacking in any substance whatsoever. In fact, editors are getting very concerned that their Kate Middleton scoops have so little flesh on them that they are actually looking anaemic.

Said one, Paul Dacres of this stuff, "Earlier this week I ended up running pieces revealing that she had worn a hat, then a coat and then a belt which she had worn once before. Tragic. This is a clear indication that our Kate features are completely starved of any real material."

"What next?," he asked, "Will we be reduced to running articles asking if Kate is too thin?"

Tonight's TV highlights:
● My Big Fat Royal Wedding
(All channels)

"We were always very close to your mother..."

Episode 94

Middle-aged man in jeans: This week we test drive the Clarkson Testerossa. Is it racier than the old Clarkson Legova or does it have more grunt than the classic Clarkson Libido?

If I put this baby through its paces, will it give me the ride of a lifetime or will the wheels come off as I go round the bend?

(Yes, we get the idea. Ed.)

YOUR EYE TEAM AT THE ABBEY

Bringing You The Very Best On Every Aspect Of The Royal Wedding Of The Century

Phil Airtime, Anchor, will be bringing you hours and hours of on-the-spot drivel. Everything from what the weather is doing to what the Daily Telegraph is saying that morning.

Glenda Slagg, Fashion Correspondent, will comment on how much she loves some women's dresses and how much she hates others before asking "arenchasick of the whole wedding?".

J.C. Flannel, Religious Editor, will explain the religious significance of the updated liturgy as and when it happens, including the big question no one is asking: "Will Kate agree to obey the Duke of Edinburgh?".

Lord Fellowes of Downton, Royal Insider, gives an Upstairs Downstairs view of who the guests really are – the Princes, the Dukes... right down to the humble Earls.

Sir Stephen Fry, Twitterer, will be tweeting from inside the Abbey with his unique take on one of the world's great state occasions (Bless!).

E.J. Thribb, the Eye's Laureate, will compose a poem to Wills and Kate live from the Abbey steps, beginning "So Farewell, Then Kate's wait...".

Dave Spart, Political Reporter, in the crowd will be giving the anarchist view, as he sprays "Fuck The Royals" on the side of the Abbey and is arrested by Inspector Knacker.

David Dimblebore will be sitting at home watching the telly and giving a live commentary to his wife about how much better he would do it than Fearne Cotton and the bloke from Formula One.

(That's enough wedding. Ed.)

Yes, don't miss the Big Eye on the Big Day!

WEDDING OF THE YEAR

RECORD APPLICATIONS FOR STREET PARTIES

by Our Marriage Staff **Michael White Dress**

AS wedding fever grips the nation, councils up and down Britain are recording a sensational number of applications for licences to hold street parties.

From Land's End to John O'Groats, the story is the same. From the Outer Hebrides to inner Croydon, Britain has responded with one voice.

Yes, a staggering zero applications have been made for joyous outdoor celebrations to mark the historic wedding of Ed Miliband and Justine Thornton.

Wed Miliband

Said a council spokesman, "It's phenomenal. We've never seen anything like it. By my reckoning, there will be no bunting, balloons or banners at all anywhere."

So as "Waity Justine" finally gets to marry her dashing politician, Ed, and the handsome young couple walk up the aisle of the registry office accompanied by their children, they will be watched by an estimated global audience of none.

Wed Balls

Bells will not be ringing out across the land, as the fairytale story of the millennium reaches its happy ending. Said one wedding expert, "It's the classic love story. Boy meets Spin Doctor. Spin Doctor tells him to get married or he won't get elected. No wonder the country hasn't taken Ed 'n' Justy to their hearts."

Not everybody, however, has been caught up in the outbreak of hysterical public apathy surrounding the wedding.

One member of the public said, "I'm not going to sit around ignoring Ed's big day. No, I'm going to leave the country for the whole week or my name is not David Miliband".

COULSON: 'I NEVER KNEW ANY OF THEM'

by Our Crime Staff **Nick Everyone**

The staff of the News of the World

THE former editor of the News of the World angrily denied that he had any knowledge of leading members of his staff when he edited the paper.

In particular he said he had never hired, met, or even heard of news editor Sid "Psycho" Noggs, a former inmate of HMP Broadmoor convicted of murder, arson and serial phone hacking.

"I've no idea who Sid is," said Coulson, "nor his colleague Len 'Razors' Krayfish who claims to have been the parliamentary correspondent during my editorship, nor even Phil 'The Wapping Strangler' Grunt who is currently serving a life sentence at HMP Wormwood Scrubs while editing the features pages."

A spokesman for the News of the World said, "We take very seriously any allegations of impropriety on the part of the paper and we will look carefully at any evidence before destroying it."

Cluff

Lives of the Saints and Martyrs No. 94
St George Sees The Light

ANDTHERE was a high-minded young man in those days called George of Monbiot whose only concern was to save the world from the evils of nuclear energy.

And he would regularly sit upon the top of his column in the Guardian, throwing stones at all those foolish enough to believe in what they called "the Greatest Power of All". But one day George was sitting in his organic plastic greenhouse when he saw that the lights were about to go out.

"There is only one way in which we can all be saved," he exclaimed to his followers: "We must all worship the power of our new god, nuclear energy".

And George's followers were so amazed at his miraculous conversion that they all with one accord hurled stones at him, calling him "bastard", "fascist" and "Judas" on the *Comment Is Free* thread.

DIARY

MY KING JAMES BIBLE

BONO

At age 12, I was a big, big fan of King Jamie's Bible. Reading the amazing story of the Sermon on the Mount, taught me something very important about myself, something very humbling, a lesson I will never forget: if you have a message, and you want to reach out to the widest number of people, then the best place to let loose that message on humanity is the largest, widest, tallest stadium you can possibly find.

Rock music has been profoundly influenced by the rich textures and language of Jimmy's Bible. You only have to think of deeply familiar phrases like "And the word was made flesh" "An eye for an eye" and "I still haven't found what I'm looking for" to realise how deeply those of us who toil in rock's vineyard have been imbued with a sense of the work's majesty.

I read it still, and identify more than ever with the Baby Jesus and all that he went through. Though I was not born in a manger – and that's something I'm learning to accept – I too have faced criticism, and I too have managed to connect, in all humility, with millions of people the world over.

SIR ANDREW MOTION

To read The King James Bible is to feel simultanaeously at home, a citizen of the world, and a traveller through eternity. Just think of the phrases it has given our language. It's a funny old world. Wham, bam, thank you ma'am. There's nowt so queer as folk. Oh, hokey-cokey-cokey. Whatever our faith, whatever we may believe, whether we believe nothing, or, better still, everything, we realise when we read The King James Bible that we are not only travellers at home but citizens of eternity, feeling through the world what it is to live simultanaeously at home and abroad, within and without, up and down, to and fro, and just as importantly, inside out.

ED BALLS

It tells us nothing whatever about the biggest fall in consumer confidence for almost 20 years, it tells us nothing about the jobs and growth we need to get the deficit down, it tells us nothing about how what's happening now in the economy is imperilling the recovery, it tells us nothing about reversing the VAT rise on fuel, and it offers no plan at all for rebuilding the economy and dealing with the competitive challenges we're going to be facing in the future. It's all very well saying it's a great book, full of beautiful language or whatever, but it's still full of the same tired old excuses, the same reckless disregard for what really matters in the here and now. In the beginning was the word, okay, I can go along with that, but not if the word tells us nothing about ensuring year-on-year growth in the marketplace.

ALAN YENTOB

I first encountered the King James Bible in the late 80s. It must have been Philip Roth who first put me on to it after I'd had lunch with Gilbert and George, and they alerted me via Keith Haring to the incredibly exciting new happenings in the world of religion, so I gave my good friend Philip Glass – do you know Phil? – a bell and he told me that the King James was truly stunning, an understated masterpiece of finely-wrought prose with a huge numbers of eminent supporters including Nick Serota and of course David (Bowie). For me, it's a book that has a hell of a lot to tell us about love and death and fish and whales, yup, it's really up there with Tracey's most recent installations and some of Salman's greatest novels.

SARAH BROWN

I've been reading the King James Bible every night with Gordon! So wonderfully uplifting and wise – and the King James Bible is good too. While flicking my way through the King James Bible last night I was wearing a gorgeous cream jacket with matching red trim by the splendid Katherine Hooker! The lovely lovely Gordon and I read the Ten Commandments, which turn out to be really great! In fact, I wish there were lots more of them as I love a big strong man telling me what to do – that's why I'm not ashamed to call myself a feminist! Terrific!

V.S. NAIPAUL

I used to enjoy The King James Bible, but I now see I was mistaken. King James is a terribly over-rated figure, and so is his Bible. The story it tells is far-fetched and the author has no idea when to stop. As a character, Adam lacks all credibility. Why should we be bothered with this dull fellow who does nothing but pick a fruit from a tree and eat it? God is even more slapdash: ruthlessly ambitious, but with no real distinction.

As told to C R A I G   B R O W N

GLENDA SLAGG

Fleet Street's Best Supporting Hackette!!!!

■ JENNI MURRAY!!! So she's now the slimline Queen of Woman's Hour!!?! Don't make us laugh, love!! OK, you've lost 3 stone and had your picture on the front of the noospaper!!?! You could have fooled me sweetheart??! If you'd lost another 30 stone we might have noticed!!?? Geddit!?!?

■ HATS OFF to Woman's Hour-glass (geddit??) Jenni Murray. Jen's had the courage to lose an amazing 3 stone and shows us the stunning results on the front page of the noospaper!?!! Gone forever is the Ten-Ton-Tessie of the airwaves!!!? Say hullo to the slinky and svelte new siren of the Sit-at-home Sisterhood!?!!

■ SALLY BERCOW!!! Doncha love her!!?! She's the Speaker's sexbomb spouse who posed naked on the top of Big Ben!!?!! Good on yer for daring to take on the Westminster stuffed-shirts with their out-dated Victorian prudery!! You're the girl who's dragged Parliament into the 21st century by showing that a woman's place is no longer in the home??! It's in a sheet at the top of Big Ben!?!?

■ SALLY BERCOW – what an outrage!!! She's the sex-crazed slapper who's brought disgrace on one of our most ancient offices of state!?!! That's the Speaker of the House of Commons, stoopid!!? What was she thinking of, taking her kit off in the hallowed precincts of Big Ben??!? No wonder her Speaker-hubby hangs his head in shame as silly Sally shows off a-poutin' and a-spoutin', a-tweetin' and a-bleatin', as if she was Lady Gaga?!!?! What a silly Bercow!!?? Geddit??!!!

Byeee!!

DIRTY DES LAUNCHES NEW MAGAZINE

SPEAKERS' WIVES

TIT
Sally makes one of herself

ARSE
Her husband looks like one

That Miliband Hyde Park Speech
What You Missed

" My fellow Americans, I have a dream, a dream of a country where women get the vote and black people can sit on buses without fear of being arrested, yes, this is the Britain we are marching towards, a Britain where slavery has been abolished and every Tolpuddle Martyr has been freed. Today I stand before you, a simple Labour leader, to join your protest against some of the cuts, though obviously not all of them because lets face it if we'd been elected we would have to have made some too... *(boos from audience)* No let me finish if it hadn't been for the previous Labour government we wouldn't be here today, hang on... *(more boos from audience)* let me finish by saluting you all and assuring you in the words of Martin Luther Kennedy, "Ich Bin Ein Milibander. "

VIOLENCE MARRED BY PEACEFUL PROTEST

No To Cuts... except for the police obviously

These anarchists are very well organised

THE ALTERNATIVE VOICE

DAVE SPART (Co-Organiser of the Dollis Hill Facebook Anarchists Against the Tory Cuts Collective)

The right-wing press have utterly, totally and predictably unleashed a barrage of sickening hypocrisy and deliberate smears against the activities of a totally peaceful group of anarchists, ie myself and my colleagues who demonstrated in non-threatening balaclavas due to the cold weather and carried heavy walking sticks for negotiating the cobbled streets, er...er...we were merely asserting our rights to forcibly occupy the citadels of capitalism and oppression such as the Ritz, Fortnum and Freemasons and, er, Ann Summers, the unacceptable face of the sexual industrial complex who objectify women as mere sexual chattels and thereby make themselves a legitimate target for peaceful acts of rioting and arson, er... small wonder the fascist police blatantly did nothing to obstruct us in our smashing up of the hated cashpoint machines of global capitalism and the spraypainting of the Nazi lions in Trafalgar Square, er...er... thereby deliberately making us look bad which is not surprising given that many of the so-called anarchists were probably undercover police officers working for MI5 such as Steve who I have never liked and who I did not want to join our collective in the first place (cont. p. 94).

DAILY TELEGRAPH | Friday, 1 April 2011

Letters to the Editor

SIR – It was distressing to read in your report of the recent riots in London that Fortnum and Mason had nothing but a basket of chocolate Easter bunnies on offer for the anarchists to tip over.

As one who remembers the old Fortum's where I was treated to tea by my uncle the Rev. Hugo Gussett before being taken back to prep school at St. Crumpets, I can recall vividly the sumptious feast that made this once proud emporium a byword for all that was finest in British afternoon comestible fare.

No one who sampled, as I did, the Knickerbocker Tory consisting of ice cream, whipped cream, clotted cream and creamed cream, all of it served in a huge glass with a cucumber sandwich, Bath Oliver biscuits, ginger preserves, gentlemen's relish, Battenberg slices and Christmas pudding will ever forget the experience.

To think that these anarchists had to put up with vulgar 'Easter bunnies' in a basket! No wonder they ran riot in protest at the decline of our once great nation.

Sir Herbert Gussett

The Old Bakery,
Much-Icing-on-Cake,
Dorset.

"Alright, have it your way – violent crime is down"

YOUR TV TONIGHT

8.00 Snøringbøre

Melancholy Swedish detective Superintendant Snøringbøre investigates the mysterious death of a gay dentist who is found dead in a disused herring factory outside the little village of Smorgasbord.

9.00 Krashingbøre

Norwegian forensic pathologist, Hedvig Krashingbøre looks into a mysterious spate of suicides, allegedly caused by the mass-depression brought on by the months of darkness in the northern winter. Or are the suicides in fact caused by watching endless depressing TV serials about Scandinavian detectives?

10.00 Børender

Based on Sven Svensson's best-selling trilogy, The Børender Triløgy, this made-for-TV serial opens with Inspector Børender overcoming his recurring bouts of depression, following an unhappy divorce, by investigating his own suicide when his body is found floating in a fjord with a note indicating that he had taken his own life rather than watch another miserable Scandinavian detective programme.

11.00 Midsømer Mörders

An unspoilt Finnish village is stunned when a Muslim Afro-Caribbean herring fisherman moves in and *(That's enough, Ed.)*

49

What You Switched Off

tv news 94

Presented by Sally Smiley and Jim Dull

Smiley: ...Thank you, Minister. And now we're going over for a live update from our man in Tripoli, Steve Clueless.

(We see man in anorak standing next to very large hole in the ground)

Smiley: Steve, can you tell us what's happening there on the ground now?

Clueless: Well, what I'm being told is that there's been a lot of bombing going on. Last night we could hear from the hotel some pretty large explosions and the sky was lit up with anti-aircraft fire.

(Repeat earlier footage of night sky lit up with tracer fire)

Smiley: And do you know what the Coalition targets were?

Clueless: No, but we're pretty sure they were military targets and that the bombing caused a lot of damage, as you can see from this hole in the ground.

(Turns to elderly Libyan man in street next to him)

Clueless: Was this a missile depot, or a strategic command and control post?

(We see interpreter shouting question at old man who looks confused)

Interpreter: He says the hole has always been here. He remembers playing in it when he was a boy. It was caused by Ronald Reagan.

Smiley: I'm sorry, Steve, we're going to have to stop you there because we're going live to Downing Street where Naomi Grimface is expecting an important announcement at any minute.

(We see woman reporter standing grim-faced outside Number Ten, looking under severe strain)

Smiley: Naomi, what's the latest on that emergency Cobra meeting?

Grimface: Well, Sally, earlier today I saw all the ministers going to the meeting, and they all looked pretty serious.

(We see repeat footage of men you don't recognise walking along street carrying files)

Grimface: The latest that I've been told is that, at any moment now, we may see Nick Clegg coming out. Ah, this may be him now.

(We see door opening a crack and small tabby cat is let out)

Jim Dull: I'm sorry, Naomi, we'll come back to you shortly. But we've just been getting some rather worrying news from Japan. We're going over live to Mike Monogloticus in Tokyo. Mike, you've

been looking at local Japanese television and I gather that something pretty serious is going on.

(Cut to film of elderly Japanese woman picking spinach)

Monogloticus: Well, what we're hearing is that radioactive spinach is making its way into Tokyo's food chain.

Dull: That sounds pretty catastrophic. I mean, there are 20 million people in Tokyo. Could they all be at risk?

Monogloticus: Well, that's the question everyone's asking. But there are some experts, like the one I saw earlier today in your package, who say that there's no real cause for alarm, because you would have eat at least 10 tons of this spinach before you would feel any ill effects.

Dull: And what about these reports of reactor 7 giving off clouds of radioactive smoke? Does that mean that it has exploded and will soon be showering deadly fall-out right across the Pacific Basin?

(We see old clip of Chernobyl followed by footage of Nagasaki in 1945)

Monogloticus: Well, I gather from the experts that the cloud you could see if we were closer to the scene may actually not be killer smoke, but only steam arising from the water that they are using to put the fires out.

Dull: And is that likely to cause massive food shortages throughout the country?

(We see film of supermarket in Libya with empty shelves)

Sally: Thank you, Mike, but we'll have to stop you there because we've got a report from the rebel-held town of Shawadiwadi, where there's apparently a terrible shortage of spinach. Over to our man in the east of Libya, Ben Ghazi.

(We see man on road next to burnt-out tank, surrounded by men in jeans firing guns into air)

Ghazi: Well, Sally, what I'm hearing is a lot of gunfire. But I have to say that, right at this moment, it's not exactly clear whether the rebel forces are advancing or retreating. But I can tell you that earlier today, when I went on a tour of the food shops of Benghazi with one of the rebel commanders, we couldn't find a single leaf of spinach anywhere.

Dull: I'm sorry, Ben, but we'll have to cut you off there because we've got a live link with the former head of the Royal Air Force, Admiral Sir Malcolm Armchair.

(We see grey-haired man in corduroys in agreeable Home Counties, struggling to get his lawn-mower to start)

Armchair: Well, the overriding lesson we learned from Gulf One was that a No Fly Zone pretty soon leads to serious "mission creep", which can land you in all sorts of hot water.

(We see repeat footage of the entire RAF [two planes] taking off from somewhere in Southern England)

Dull: So we're going to assassinate Gaddafi, is that what you're suggesting?

Armchair: Good heavens, no. The UN resolution makes it absolutely clear that our job is only to fly 1,500 miles out to Libya – because we haven't got any aircraft carriers – and then not to drop any of these very expensive missiles, just in case there might be a few civilians about, and then fly safely home to Blighty to fill up with petrol which has got jolly expensive lately because of all this nonsense going on in the Middle East, which we keep on seeing far too much of on the television, if you ask me...

Smiley: ...Thank you, Admiral. And now, back to Downing Street, where we're hearing that the all-important Cobra meeting may be coming to an end and that very soon now we may be seeing Nick Clegg coming out of that door to give us an update.

(We see Grimface still standing outside Number Ten, where the door remains firmly shut)

Grimface: Thank you, Sally, and I have to tell you that this meeting of Cobra has already been going on for several hours. Earlier we did see the door open, but all we saw was the famous Downing Street cat, Al-Jazeera.

(Repeat of footage showing cat being let out of door by unseen hand [possibly SamCam])

Smiley: Naomi, do we have any word of whom Nick Clegg has been talking to at the Cobra meeting. I mean, is it possible that he was on the phone to President Sarkozy or President Obama? Or that he was ordering a secret SAS hit squad to take out Col. Gaddafi by using deadly radioactive spinach?

Grimface: Well, I'm hoping to be able to put that question directly to Nick Clegg, as soon as he comes out of that door.

Dull: Naomi, sorry, I'm going to have to cut you off there because we're just getting some very sad news in from Germany where it seems that a polar bear cub called Knut has very sadly died.

Smiley: Do we know whether he was killed by a Coalition missile, or had he possibly been fed radioactive spinach by Japanese tourists? We have on the line the editor of the well-known German magazine Bears Und Bearmen, Herr Bear.

(We see bearded man in anorak standing outside zoo)

Herr Bear *(for it is he)*: Zis is a very sad day for all ze world. I blame global warming.

(We see footage of jet planes taking off, tracer bullets in night sky, exploding reactors, woman picking spinach and door of Ten Downing Street remaining closed)

Continues for 94 days...

'NO HIDING PLACE FOR TYRANTS!'
Hague's Chilling Threat

by Our Diplomatic Staff **Mojo Mowlam**

TERROR last night gripped the world's most feared dictators as they reeled under a savage attack from Britain's Foreign Secretary, Sir Winston Hague.

In an astonishing tirade, Sir William warned the world's top autocrats that their days were numbered and that very soon they would all be consigned to the dustbin of history.

William The Bonkerer

Speaking at the annual dinner of the League of Democratic African Dictators, Hague told his audience, "Unless you all introduce free and fair elections, an independent judiciary, and a free press, we shall send in all our fighter planes to bomb you to smithereens, as we are doing to Colonel Gaddafi".

There were immediate reports of mass panic among the world's dictator community.

In North Korea, President Kim Jung-Il retreated into his nuclear banker.

In Tehran President Ahmedinajad sobbed openly on state television, pleading for mercy.

In Harare, the whereabouts of President Mugabe were unknown, although later Mr Hague said he had been reliably informed that the Zimbabwean leader had fled to Venezuela.

STOP PRESS

The Foreign Office last night issued a clarification of Mr Hague's threat to destroy all the world's autocratic rulers with a poor human rights' record. The statement explained that the Foreign Secretary had not of course been referring to any of Britain's allies, such as the rulers of Bahrain, Qatar, Saudi Arabia and the People's Republic of China.

Tyrant Using Human Shields

THERE ARE shocked reports coming in that struggling despot David Cameron has been using Liberal Democrats as "human shields".

"They're being cynically placed around Mr Cameron to stop any attacks on him," said a man in camouflage fatigues.

Mr Cameron denied he was using Liberal Democrats as human shields, saying they were much more useful as an occasional table. *(Reuters)*

"OK, now give me your mother's maiden name and place of birth"

WHAT IS HAPPENING IN YEMEN, SYRIA, EGYPT?

We don't know.

THAT ALL IMPORTANT ARAB INVOLVEMENT IN THE COALITION

❶ **All civilians killed will be Arabs**

❷ **Er...**

❸ **That's it.**

WHO ARE THEY – THOSE LIBYAN REBEL LEADERS?

SHUFTI AL-MUFTI Member of the transitional National Resistance Council for a Free Libya. Al-Mufti was previously head of Gaddafi's key International Security Directorate, but is now a firm believer in freedom, democracy and himself being allowed to continue in power.

OSAMA BIN-GHAZI Formerly a full-time volunteer in the Islamic Jihadi Brotherhood organisation, and a frequent traveller to Afghanistan, Pakistan and Iraq, Bin-Ghazi is now a firm believer in freedom, democracy and the imposition of Sharia law on the whole of Libya.

MOHAMMED AL ANORAQ This former East London minicab driver is now a General in the rebels' 1st Non-Armoured Division, and when he is not being interviewed by Channel 4 News because he speaks English, spends his time driving up and down the coast road in his Toyota truck, hoping that the Coalition will hurry up and win the war for him and his friends.

THOSE OPERATION NAME SUGGESTIONS IN FULL

● **Operation Odyssey Dawn**

● **Operation French Dawn**

● **Operation 2011 A Space Odyssey**

● **Operation David Bowie's A Space Oddity**

● **Operation Bill Oddiessey's Arab Springwatch**

● **Operation Dawning-on-us-this-wasn't-a-very-good idea-after-all**

(That's enough names, Ed)

HAGUE: YET ANOTHER SHOCK THREAT TO GADDAFI

'Our Boys Would Go In If We Had Any'

by Our Lack of Defence Staff **Robert Foxed**

BRITAIN's Foreign Secretary, William Hague, yesterday warned the embattled Libyan leader that Britain is now ready to commit its entire armed forces to ensuring that the civilians of Benghazi are free to overthrow Col. Gaddafi if they so wish by their own efforts.

Firstly, Mr Hague ordered a massive air strike by the entire RAF, 3 Tornados. But before taking off, the pilots were unfortunately informed that they had all been made redundant under the new Defence Spending Programme.

Secondly, Mr Hague ordered the entire Royal Navy, HMS Superfluous, to float up and down off the Libyan coast in a menacing manner. Unfortunately, the rowing boat in question had already been sent to the scrapyard under the Defence Spending Programme.

Thirdly, Mr Hague trenchantly refused to rule out sending in the entire British Army to give "non-military support" to the rebels in eastern Libya.

Unfortunately, the two soldiers not currently employed in Afghanistan had been discharged from their regiments under the Defence Spending Programme.

"Never fear," Sir Winston Hague told the House of Commons, "if this conflict in Libya carries on until 2020, by then we will have two enormous aircraft carriers which we can deploy to the Mediterranean, so long as we have worked out whether we can afford to equip them with any planes."

Sources close to Col. Gaddafi said that he was studying Mr Hague's statement very carefully, and that when he had completed the reconquest of his country, he would give a reply.

Obama's Shock Threat To Gaddafi

'Our Boys Are Coming Out'
(p. 24)

"It's always difficult to get tickets for the men's 100 metres, I don't know why"

Those Olympic events Boris couldn't get tickets for

The High Jump (after your wife finds you sent flowers and champagne to some hot totty who has a flat off the King's Road)

The 100 Metres Dash (out of the totty's flat in the hope of avoiding the papps)

The Cycling Time Trial (working out how quickly you can cycle there and back to the hot totty's flat and still convince the wife you've popped out for a pint of milk)

The Marathon (Twenty-six miles is how far you'll have to run to escape wife's wrath if the hot totty gets a bun in the oven)

(That's enough Boris Olympics events, Ed.)

DAILY TELEGRAPH | Friday, 15 April 2011

Letters to the Editor
Britain and its African legacy

SIR – The recent attempts to rake up some sort of scandal over this country's colonial record are a sad sign of the age in which we live.

As one who was privileged to serve in British Kenyattaland (subsequently the People's Republic of Kenyanyika) I was able to see at first hand the benefits of enlightened western rule in this sadly under developed part of the world.

Let us not forget that the Mao Mao uprising was a communist led plot amongst the Kikillyu tribe designed to instigate the mass murder of the entire British Community living in Happy Valley. Had the leader of the revolt Mr. Jomo Machete (later President Machete) had his way not one of us would have escaped ritual dismemberment at the hands of voodoo witch doctors.

However when apprehended, the perpetrators of these abominable atrocities were treated with traditional courtesy and fair play by their British captors. If being given a cup of tea and a free copy of the Illustrated London News is now to be categorised as torture and a war crime, then yes, we must plead guilty.

If, however, a sane historical perspective is to be maintained we should perhaps remember that the alleged events happened a very long time ago and that nothing can now be gained from dragging up the unreliable memories of old men some of them suffering from dementia, as so many of us are.

Sir Herbert Gusset
Happy Valley,
East Grinstead.

"Philosophers Sans Frontières – we're here to bring you a new world view"

POETRY CORNER

**In Memoriam
Brian Haw, Peace Campaigner**

So. Farewell
Then
Brian Haw.

You camped outside
Parliament for
Many years

Protesting about
The War in
Iraq.

But now
You have been moved
On for good.

E.J. Thribb (17½)

**In Memoriam
Monty Sunshine, jazz
clarinettist**

So. Farewell
Then
Monty Sunshine,
Jazz Clarinettist.
Petite Fleur

That was your
Number One hit.

Yes, truly
It can be said
That the sunshine
Has gone out
Of our lives.

E.J. Thribb (17½ r.p.m.)

**In Memoriam
Elizabeth Taylor**

So. Farewell
Then
Liz Taylor.
Hollywood Goddess
And star of the
Silver Screen.

You married
Eight times
Including
The same man twice.

Now, alas, you
Have literally
Gone for a
Burton.

E.J. Thribb (17½ husbands)

AV – How It Works

An Eye Guide To The Voting System They're All Talking About

by Hugh Gov

AV is the simplest voting system imaginable. Think of it like this: you are going into a sweetshop and you want to buy a Mars Bar. You've always bought Mars Bars because you feel at home with them and they've been your choice of confectionery since you were old enough to go into a sweet shop. But then you find that the shopkeeper won't allow you to have a Mars Bar, your preferred option, and offers you a Twix.

You quite like Twix, though not as much as you like Mars Bars. But you really hate Bounty because it's got coconut in. So you agree that Twix is your second preference.

Imagine your horror when the shopkeeper goes to his computer and, after two days, tells you that because most of the other Mars Bar supporters have switched not to Twix but to Bounty, the country is now going to be run by the brand of chocolate bar you least like.

That's why my first preference in this referendum would be to vote "Yes", but my second would be to vote "No". This should ensure that at least I get a Kit-Kat when the votes have been counted.

TV – How It Works

Voters choose to stay at home and watch the television rather than go to the polling station and vote.

AV's ok... but it wouldn't be my first choice

TV Highlights

To AV and AV Not

FILM noir classic. Harry Morgan (Humphrey Bogart) is simply trying to make a living on the Nazi-occupied island of Martinique in the Second World War. But when he meets "Slim" Browning (Lauren Bacall), a fiery election reform campaigner who wants to escape the island and take the AV movement all the way to Berlin, he joins their side. Will they make it out?

I AV a Dream

FULL replay of Martin Luther King's speech – arguably the greatest of the twentieth century – in which he decries the iniquities of the First Past the Post system. "I have a dream that my four little children will one day live in a nation where they will not be judged by the colour of their skin but by the slightly different voting system they have decided will, in the long run, be slightly fairer, or, at the very least, marginally less unfair."

Those AV Arguments in Full

Yes to AV campaign

MPs work harder to earn and keep our support.
Your next MP would have to aim to get more than 50 percent of the vote to be sure of winning.

A bigger say on who your local MP is.
Ranking candidates gives you more say in who comes first and who comes last.

Tackling the 'jobs for life' culture.
Too many MPs have 'safe seats' for life. Force complacent politicians to sit up and listen.

No to AV campaign

"What are we running for? For me, it's Cancer Research this year"

Lines on the Electoral Triumph of the Scottish National Party

By WILLIAM REES-MCGONAGALL

'Twas in the year of Two Thousand and Eleven
That Alex Salmond thought he must be in Heaven.
He was the brave leader of the victorious SNP
Who turned the Labour vote in Scotland from large to wee.
From Berwick-on-Tweed to John o' Groats,
No one had ever won so many votes.
No wonder Bold Alex was feeling sae gay,
As he witnessed the defeat of Labour Leader Mr Grey.
"At last," he declared, "Scotland has thrown off the shackles,"
A comment that in England raised not a few hackles.
"Next step" he cried is full independence
And his bonny face glowed with a heavenly transcendence.
"No more Sassenachs telling us what to do,
In future we'll make our own decisions och aye the noo."
He continued in this vein for many an hour,
Droning on, like a bagpipe, about gaining supreme power.
And so his first decision was to "let the people choose"
In a referendum that given past experience he was almost certainly bound to lose.

© W. Rees-McGonagall

PHONE HACKING SCANDAL 'IRRELEVANT' SAYS MINISTER

by Our Political Staff **Robert Pest**

CULTURE Secretary, Mr Jeremy Hunt, yesterday dismissed attempts to link the News of the World phone hacking scandal to Rupert Murdoch's bid for full control of BSkyB.

He told Sky News, in an exclusive interview, "I fail to see what possible bearing criminal activity by Mr Murdoch's newspaper could have on his TV company. The two issues are quite clearly separate, apart from the fact that Mr Murdoch controls both of them."

He continued, in another exclusive interview with the Sunday Times, "The fact that Mr Murdoch has been illegally bugging my predecessor as Culture Secretary is entirely irrelevant to my decision to award him full control of BSkyB and anything else he wants."

He concluded, in a specially written article for the News of the World, "I have a high regard for Rupert Murdoch. Few men have done more for Britain than Mr Murdoch. It is only right and fitting that he should now be rewarded for his selfless and constant support for our great party, I mean country."

© *News International 2011.*

DOCTOR, I'M CONFUSED BY THE CHANGES TO THE NHS

THERE'S A LOT OF IT ABOUT

'I WAS NOT HACKED'
Admits Shaken Celebrity

by Our Media Staff **Phil Space**

A WELL-KNOWN celebrity who cannot be named for legal reasons (ie, you haven't heard of him) admitted last night that his phone had at no stage been hacked by News of the World journalists.

He told police, "When I read nothing about myself in the paper, it finally dawned on me that something peculiar was going on.

"I contacted Scotland Yard to complain and was told that they were not interested. The officer told me that there were thousands of celebrities who were not on the list and I would just have to take my turn."

The celebrity continued, "It was a shocking lack of intrusion into my private life. I am looking for compensation in the region of £100,000 at the very least, or maybe I will settle for a small mention in the TV column."

AN APOLOGY
by Gnome International, Publishers of the Gnomes of the World

We would like unreservedly to apologise for our previous behaviour in relation to voice mail interception.

In the past, over a number of years, we have steadfastly attempted to cover up the widespread and entirely authorised culture of illegal snooping, which was prevalent at the Gnomes of the World.

We are very sorry that this did not work and, in particular, we regret that our attempt to claim that this was all the work of "a single rogue journalist" failed to convince anyone, due to the fact that it was not true.

We further would like to record our genuine regret that our attempts to buy off a number of prominent personalities with large cheques were likewise unsuccessful.

It is now our sincere hope that this fulsome yet vague apology, combined with yet further payments to people who might otherwise make trouble, will be enough to put an end to this embarrassing story and enable the News of the Gnomes to continue to uphold the finest traditions of investigative journalism and the legitimate exposure of unsavoury public figures who are acting against the public interest by bringing spurious criminal cases against Gnome International in the hope of making a quick buck.

We assure them that we know not only where they live, but who they are talking to and who has left them a message recently.

© *Gnome International, April 2011*

The Eye's Controversial New Columnist
He knows nothing, and he's not afraid to say it

I notice a so-called newspaper has reported the nonsense about News of the World journalists getting arrested. This makes me extremely angry. Typical so-called 'knee jerk' reporting. Just what is so bad about being covertly listened to? I don't know of any chaps down at my local nursery who haven't been monitored by listening devices at some time or other, and it hasn't done them any harm. I'm sure all these journalists were innocently doing was making sure John Prescott wasn't hungry, and to check if he needed a breast to suck on. He should thank them for *(cont. p. 94)*

Those Controversial Interns in Full

NICK CLEGG: Got first proper job thanks to his father putting in a word with his friend.

HAROLD STEPTOE: Given a lucrative job in his father's rag-and-bone business in spite of the fact that other candidates may have been better qualified.

LUKE SKYWALKER: Inherited considerable skills from his biological father Darth Vader, who gave him unfair assistance in his struggle to kill the Emperor and bring peace to the entire galaxy.

THE QUEEN, Elizabeth II: Understood to have got her job from her father after he 'put in a good word' for her with the entire nation.

JESUS CHRIST: Sent down to earth as his father's representative, following no clear interview procedure and *(that's enough Ed)*

"I'm hoping this will lead to a real job"

New Coat of Arms for Miss Middleton

by Our Armorial Staff the late Sir Hugh Montgomery-Massivesnob,
Rouge Pursuivant to the Royal College of Heralds

MISS MIDDLETON's choice of symbolism for her coat of arms reflects the wide variety of her interests and the distinguished family background from which she is descended.

The main quartering of the shield shows:

1. A mountain rampant to illustrate her family's love of social climbing (*surely her love of skiing? Ed*)
2. A pair of cabin doors argent carrying the legend 'set to manual', to illustrate Miss Middleton's mother's services to the airline industry
3. A transom of party 'blowouts'

in azure and vert, illustrating Mr Middleton's services to the children's party entertainment industry
4. A packet of Marlboro cigarettes in gules and white, a playful reference to the new Princess's education at the distinguished public school of that name.

The embrasure is to be mounted with an hourglass to signify Miss Middleton's patience over the years with the whole gorged and collected with a surround of oak leaves and acorns to commemorate the public house in which the couple first met, the Royal Oak and Ferret, St Andrews.

"So you must be 'vegetarian, non-smoker, amateur artist, likes Wagner'?"

ROYAL WEDDING
Notes & queries

Is Mrs Carole Middleton (née Goldsmith) related to the late Sir James Goldsmith?

(Mrs Sharon Snellgove)

Yes, there is a link between Mrs Middleton and the late Sir James, leader of the now alas disbanded Referendum Party and father of the civil rights activist Jemima Khan. My own research on the invaluable internet site *howtheyarerelated.com* clearly shows that the late grocery tycoon's great-great-great-grandfather, Herr Otto von Fishpaste-Goldschmidt, who lived in the Schwabian town of Bad Marmeit in 1828 married his first cousin Elsa Mittelton-Goldschmidt, who, it turns out, is the four-times great-aunt twice removed of none other than Carole Middleton, the mother of the future Queen of England. Amazing or what?

Reginald Nerdsley (né Goldschmidt), Solihull

Mr Nerdsley is woefully mistaken with his fanciful tales about long-forgotten Germans. Anyone who has a passing acquaintance with the history of English literature and does not waste their time on ill-informed internet sites will know that Sir James, the eminent financier and philanthropist, had no connection with Germany, but was of Irish descent and could claim as his fifteenth cousin six times removed the distinguished Anglo-Irish dramatist and poet Sir Oliver Goldsmith, known to his friends (who included Dr Johnson) as "Jammy" or "Fishpaste". Mrs Middleton, on the other hand, can trace her ancestry no further back than 1794, to a foundling who was taken in by the Worshipful Company of Goldsmiths, and was given their name as a token of their benevolence. To suggest any familial connection between the erstwhile proprietor of *Now* magazine and the mother of our future Queen

is so absurdly wide of the mark that I am astonished that your once-respected newspaper should give it any space at all.

Rev. Ethel Fantoni (née Goldsmith)

Is it true that Prince Charles has now become the longest-serving heir to the throne in British history?

Col. A. J. Frisbee (Retd)

Technically, this may be true, in that the history of Britian only goes back to the Act of Union in 1707. Prior to that date, however, we must recall Ethelbert the Green who, in the 8th Century, reached the ripe old age of 94 before he finally succeeded his mother Elizaburga to the throne of the Kingdom of Mercia. As legend has it, she was determined to remain alive for as long as possible, due to her conviction that if her foolish and peevish son were to succeed, the royal house would soon fall and the kingdom would be overrun by barbarians. As it happened, no sooner had the aged and revered Queen breathed her last at the age of 143, than her son was so overjoyed at finally reaching his life's goal that he choked to death on a celebratory glass of his own organic mead. To the universal joy of his subjects, he was succeeded as King by his son Prince Willsfred and his popular wife, Katherine of Middlesex, who was herself, according to the Venerable Bede, a close relative of the powerful German Goldschmidt dynasty, which ruled over the principality of Bad Marmeit.

Sir William Shawcross, KCVO, OBN

Answers please to the following:

What does the "L" of L. Ron Hubbard stand for? How did the new Nigerian leader Goodluck Jonathan get his name? Is it true that Nick Ross is the father of Jonathan Ross?

ROYAL WEDDING MART

Royal Wedding Mug Family Tree

AT LAST! You can display all your Royal Wedding mugs in descending genealogical order! From King George VI and Lady Elizabeth Bowes-Lyons right down to Kate 'n' Wills!!

From the makers of TV's *Whose Mug Do You Think You are?*, this hand-carved wooden wedding memento is a lasting tea-based reminder of our Royal heritage. **Price: £27.42**

Comes in choice of wood: Lesley Ash, Ken Pine, Yew Laurie.

The Princess Diana Hologram Projector

Now YOU can create the effect of Princess Diana looking down on the Royal Wedding from heaven in your own living room! Simply point the projector at your ceiling, switch on and the Princess of Hearts will smile approvingly from the grave!

Plays theme tune from Oscar-winning hit Royal movie "The King's Speech"

£2,999 (from Harrods only)

Past Times

TURN YOUR PLASMA TV ROOM INTO WESTMINSTER ABBEY!

Step back in history, as you take your place in this authentic medieval Abbey pew. Made from English oak-style MDF in the village of Midsomer Middleton, this seat from by-gone years will transport you into the front row of the nation's premier religious venue from the Middle Ages.

Flat pack self-assembly
Colours: Ethel Red, Prince Black, Lady Jane Grey

Price: £473.99 (or 27 Golden Guineas)

Yes! It's the Royal Wedding BURQINI

£743.42

Don't get dangerously exposed to the sun's harmful rays as you wait on the Royal Mall for Wills 'n' Kate to appear on the balcony!

Now you can stay UV-free in this fashionable yet discreet Nigella-style Royal Wedding Burqini! You can even go for a dip in the fountains with the modesty of your shapely curves intact!!

Choice of colours: BLACK

The Official ROYAL WEDDING TROUSERPRESS

Do not settle for cheap imitations – this is the one and only authorised Royal Wedding trouserpress personally approved by Buckingham Palace and Middleton Party-poppers Plc.

This limited edition X378 WRINKLEMASTER EXECUTIVE will keep *your* creases razor sharp whilst simultaneously celebrating the wedding of the millennium.

Plays D.I.V.O.R.C.E. by Tammy Wynette

Price: £999.99

---

theguardian

Friday 13.05.11

Only Very Few Millions Turn Out For Royal Wedding

See our special 94-page picture supplement of the wedding that no one was interested in.

Plus
Polly Toynbee "The empty and tedious charade that spells the end for the monarchy".

Plus
Marina Hyde on what Polly Toynbee was wearing as she stayed home instead of going to the Royal Wedding. Were those shoes a mistake?

Plus 100s of Royal Pix and Pieces

What You Missed

BBC1 11.94 am

Huw Edwards *(for, alas, it is he)*: ...and now someone pretty important seems to be arriving, and some people are blowing trumpets. It's an elderly woman in yellow getting out of a carriage, and with her is an old gentleman in naval uniform – they're a very sprightly-looking pair, obviously enjoying Wills and Kate's big day. They might be foreign dignitaries, perhaps the Ambassador for Zimbabwe or the King of Tonga... oh, and I've just been told by my producer that the couple in question are apparently Her Majesty the Queen and the Duke of Edinburgh, who are, of course, related by marriage to the Middletons of Buckleberry... and now everyone's looking up to see the glorious sight of the Battle of Britain fly-past. You can hear the roar of those legendary aircraft which saved Britain all those years ago, the Typhoons and the Tornados... Oh no, my producer's just told me that it's a Ryanair flight heading for Ibiza... Still, it makes a stirring sight on this unforgettable day of pomp and pageantry shot through with informality and humour... and my producer tells me that we're now going over live to David Dimbleby who's sitting at home with his family, but who might have some idea of what on earth is going on and who all these people are... *(cont. for 94 hours)*

WACKO JACKO REVISITED

Special Royal Wedding Frocks!

IT'S ROYAL WEDDING TIME...
and our fashion editor **LIZ BONES** crowns the best gowns and deposes the drabbest dresses!

ER... what? This dull outfit makes Liz look a Monarch of the **glum**! It's a real ma'am-ite choice – just **throne** together! What's with the yellow, your Maj? You look like a **royale with cheese**!!

What an **anthem** idea! A pretty outfit means that **Liz** is more! Any Blue-blooded man will ex-**sceptre** in this naughty look!

Kate Middleton's slender silky number is to **Di** for! It makes me **Queen** with envy! It certainly shows that where there's a **Wills** there's a way!

Aisle have to say, we should draw a veil over Katie's frumpy frock! Having a (**middle**) **ton** of lace on show makes her look a really **weighty** Katie!!

God **nose** why Ms Tomkinson wore this! This ugly blue dress means it's **Tara** to tastefulness! I take real ex-**septum** to this kind of look!

Tara! This simple elegance proves that if it ain't **coke**, don't fix it! This proves that she's my **snort** of girl!

Get a **pip**, sis! Pippa's shameless attention grabber makes me **bridal** with annoyance! **Honour**-stly, girl, put them away, you've **maid** an ass of yourself!

Pippa-hip-hooray! Kate's sister shows off her **sibling** (sizzling) figure in this subtle dress! I **regal-ly** await her next appearance!

Holy hell! No one can say he doesn't **consecrate** on his wardrobe! He **mitre** be **anglican** for attention, but this gorgeous ensemble gets the highest **praise** from me!

What the **flock** is he playing at? Doesn't he know that pointy hats are so **old testament**? This gaudy, fussy outfit has just ruined the whole day!!

Here's a look I'd rather **Ferg**-et! Didn't she have a mirror **andy**? What is it supposed to be? **York** guess is as good as mine!

This Princess is the **Be-atrice** and end all of fashion! This daring eye-catching creation makes her look a right **Royal Knock-out!**

Hack to the drawing board, Liz! This mutton-dressed-as- **lame** ensemble will have **mails** reaching for their vomit bags on a **daily** basis!!

Has she gone to the charity shop for this? It looks like **Liz the seconds** to me! **Column** on girl, make an effort, you tragic old (*You are fired, Ed.*)

58

Letters to the Editor

The Royal Wedding

SIR – I am sure that I am not alone among the millions of delighted viewers of the Royal Wedding in being sadly disappointed by the shocking failure of the Prime Minister's wife, Mrs Samantha Cameron, to wear a hat for the ceremony in Westminster Abbey. I doubt whether in the entire history of Royal Weddings has there been such an appalling lapse in etiquette. Had this been the wife of a Labour politician (none of whom, happily, were invited this time), such a lamentable breach of ancient protocol might be understandable. Such a person would not have been brought up to know better. But Mrs Cameron, we are assured, comes from one of our leading landed families and, like her husband, had the benefit of a first-class private education. For her to fail to observe the most basic of dress codes on such an occasion, is truly unforgivable and a deplorable dereliction of duty which for me entirely ruined the whole occasion.

Lady Letitia Gusset
The Old Hattery,
Hatfield, Hats.

SIR – Like millions of others, I was moved to tears by the pageantry and splendour of the Royal Wedding, which has once again restored the nation's faith in its First Family. The service, the procession, the fly-past, all was yet another flawless demonstration of what Britain can do so much better than any other nation in the world. Only one tiny flaw in the spectacle completely spoiled for me the whole occasion. Namely the poor quality of the waving by the bride and groom as their coach passed through the loyal and cheering crowds. If only Her Late Majesty the Queen Mother (about whom, incidentally, I had the honour to write a best-selling book, still happily on sale) had still been with us, she would have instructed the young couple in the art of controlled, wide-angle, relaxed waving to the crowd, rather than the nervous, jerky and fluttering gestures of which we saw far too much on a day which for that reason alone is, alas, best forgotten.

Sir Hugo Vickers
The Old Vickerage,
Shorecross St. William, Beds.

SIR – Did Prince Harry's toast to Miss Pippa Middleton, the chief bridesmaid, include the phrase "Bottoms up"? I and the rest of the admiring male population of Britain would certainly hope so!

Mike Giggler
Via email.

Royal Wedding Lookalike Special

Frog Prince & Miss Piggy

Duke & Duchess of Cambridge

Cherub

Bridesmaid

International Rescue

Air Sea Rescue

Tinky Winky

Laa Laa

Po

I'M RIGHT. YOU'RE WRONG. SHUT UP. THE END.

NO

YES

RGJ

That climate change debate in full

The Egyptian People An Apology

IN RECENT months our reports on the so-called Arab Spring may have given readers the impression that we regarded the Egyptian people as essentially mature peace-loving democrats who were throwing off the yoke of military dictatorship in order to embrace a new secular future on a liberal western model. Headlines, such as "Egypt Joins the Modern World", "New Dawn Over the Nile" and "Sod Off Mubarak You Bastard", may have reinforced this interpretation of events.

We now realise that such a picture might have been unduly optimistic and that in fact the Egyptian populace consists largely of over-excited religious lunatics who like nothing better than inter-communal violence and setting fire to churches. Recent headlines, such as "Rampaging Mob Out of Control", "Cairo Ablaze – Death on the Nile" and "Come Back Mubarak All is Forgiven", have, we hope, redressed the balance in our coverage.

We would like to apologise for any confusion caused to our readers by our earlier reports.

© All Newspapers.

DEIRDRE SPART (Co-Chair of the Tufnell Park Fuck The Royal Wedding and Friends of the Badger Cooperative)

Once again, David Cameron has shown the Fascist reality behind his seemingly suave façade when he sickeningly told the universally-respected Socialist lesbian Ms Eagle to "Calm down, dear", the notorious catchphrase of the Fascist reactionary film-maker Michael Winner, acting as paid spokesman for the multi-national global capitalist insurance complex cartel... er... there are no more blatantly mysoginistic, patronising, patriarchalist words in the entire English language than those which the Bullingdonian public school hooray Cameron used to denigrate half of the human race, ie women, in the person of Ms Eagle. This government pretends to be opposed to racism and other hate crimes, yet its leader feels free to indulge in totally sickening verbal rape of one of our most (cont. p. 94)

BOB DYLAN'S SELL-OUT CHINA TOUR

♪ *All Along the Heavily Guarded Watchtower* ♫

♪ *Swingin' in the Wind* ♫

♪ *The Crimes They Aren't A-Changin'* ♪

"Tut! Some people! First bit of warm weather..."

IN THE COURTS

XYZ vs Ms Titzi Slapper. Before Mr Justice Cockleady. Day 94.

Sir Ephraim Hugefee QC: My Lord, I represent Mr XYZ, who is a world-famous household name.

Justice Cockleady: I have never heard of him.

Sir Ephraim Hugefee: I am indebted to Your Honour, but let me assure you that he is a familiar face on the televisual device and his name would be recognised in public houses and betting shops across the land.

Cockleady: But not in the Garrick Club, I wager.

Hugefee: Ha ha ha ha, Your Honour! But if I may return to the *res ipsa*, the appalling invasion of my client's privacy by Ms Slapper, a topless model who...

Justice Cockleady *(interrupting)*: Are there photographs available to help us focus on this grotesque invasion of privacy?

Hugefee: Indeed there are m'lud. I refer you to Bundle XXX.

Cockleady: Phew! Is it me or is it hot in here? Perhaps the usher would be so good as to open the window.

(Usher opens window)

Hugefee: I submit, m'lud, that were Ms Slapper's allegations against my client to be made public, not only would Mr XYZ become the subject of widespread ridicule and shame, but his children would be subjected to merciless bullying for the rest of their natural lives...

Cockleady: I'm terribly sorry, Sir Hugefee, I missed all that, I was still catching up with the contents of Bundle XXX.

Hugefee: Very good, My Lord. Your attention to detail is wholly admirable. I was just talking of the children, Your Honour, who surely have the basic human right to know nothing about their parents for their entire lives.

Cockleady: Indeed, that is a powerful argument, Sir Hugefee. There can be no greater freedom for children than the freedom to be spared the truth about their errant parents, whomsoever they may be – be they televisual celebrities, Premium League footballers or even members of the Bench, such as myself.

(Judge puts on black cap)

I hereby grant an order of *Gaggendum Absolutum Superinjunctionem* to be applied *contra mundum*

and to last *ad infinitum.*

(Court gasps at severity of lunatic judgement)

Hugefee: I am indebted to you, My Lord, and indeed to Mr XYZ for his speedy settlement of my very large fees.

Cockleady: I also rule that any person or persons who refer to Mr XYZ or his wife or his children or his dog or his hamster in any context whatsoever shall be taken from here to a place where they shall be hung by the neck and subjected to legitimate waterboarding techniques by trained officers of the Intelligence Services.

As to Ms Slapper, there is no restriction on publication of her name or indeed her phone number, which perhaps you could provide me for the record?

I would remind all those present that this hearing never took place and is embargoed for the next 100 years, *nemo exemptio*, in all territories including the United States of America, Antarctica and outer space.

And now it is time for luncheon, is it not?

Mr Hugefee: Indeed it is, Your Lordship.

Mr Cockleady: Perhaps this one should be on you, Sir Ephraim?

Mr Hugefee: Ha ha ha ha.

(To be continued every day for ever)

"Is it a bird? Is it a plane? No, it's SUPERINJUNCTION"

ME AND MY SPOON

THIS WEEK

SUPERINJUNCTED PUBLIC FIGURE XMC

How many spoons do you own?

That's a private matter.

When did you buy your first spoon?

None of your business.

Do you prefer soup spoons or teaspoons?

You are not allowed to know that.

Do you have a favourite spoon?

This is an outrageous invasion of my privacy. You'll be hearing from my lawyers imminently.

Have you ever used a spoon to abuse a position of trust?

There is no public interest in any of this.

Why did you volunteer to do this newspaper interview?

I'm not telling you.

Has anything amusing ever happened in connection with you and a spoon?

No.

NEXT WEEK: *Ryan Giggs – 'Me and my Gigs'*

SLAPPER IN INJUNCTION CASE

Everyone knows I'm gagging for it

IS TRUMP'S HAIR GENUINE?
Obama demands proof

by Our US Staff **Justin Wigg**

IN A shock challenge to his political rival Donald Trump, President Obama publicly questioned the origins of the tycoon's hair.

"Is it genuine or is it fake?" he asked before demanding a certificate of authenticity from Mr Trump's official hairdresser 'Weaves 'R' Us'.

Donald Trump was however furious that the integrity of his hair was being called into question.

"This hair is 100% American," he said, "it was born here – though admittedly on someone else's head."

"This thing is making me look ludicrous," said Donald Trump's hair as it *(cont. p. 94)*.

Pseudo Names Pseudo Names

...It amazes us that such a learned English publication as Private Eye has never had any Shakespearean contributions to Pseudo Names.

TAMARA and
TAMARA and TAMARA.

...Glad to see you'd heard from Tamara and Tamara and Tamara about Shakespearean Pseudo Names (Letters 1275). We'd have been in touch before ourselves, but have been busy trying to swap some land we own for a sustainable means of transport.

MIKE ING
DOM FARRER-HAWSE.

...Surely Pseudo Names has now run its course. And as for Tamara and Tamara and Tamara's suggestion that there should be Shakespearean contributions – well, they know what they can do.

X. ZITPER
SUE D'BIABERE.

...Tamara and Tamara and Tamara will no doubt be surprised at the amount of readers rushing to show they have stomach to this fight. Cry God! For Harry! And St George!

WAYNE SMORUNTU
D. BREECH (DEAR FRIENDS)
and STEPHEN D. SINUSE
SIMON AP DERBLUD.

...With yet another huge crisis needing to be sorted out here in Greece we really haven't time for made up Shakespearean names. But good luck with them anyway.

T. MONNOV
ATHENS.

...I fully agree with the Tamara triplets in the last issue, simply not enough Shakespeare in the Pseudo Names...

ELSIE KNORR.

...We really must rise to the challenge thrown down by the three Tamaras re the lack of Shakespearean contributions. This is a grave lack, and we will have to dig deep.

ALICE PORYORIK
I. NEWIMWELL.

...Shakespearean Pseudo Names, take a bow. Why – all the world's a stage, innit?

ANNE ALDERMEN
ANN D'WIMMIN
MARY-LEE PLAYERS.

...We look forward to our collective creativity.

WERTHER PRICE
OVERK IZMAN.

...I always said something will turn up, but Shakespearean names? What the Dickens is going on?

(MR) MICK ORBER.

...I agree with your previous correspondents, the three Tamaras, that more Shakespearean references need to be in the Eye.

TOBY ARNOTT OBE.

...Shakespeare in Private Eye? Over our dead bodies!

T. RESTIS, CY LENZ.

...Oh yeah, here we go again! Is there no end to your smart-arse readers and their endless and oh so clever made up names? Now they're trying to impress us by showing off with their knowledge of poxy Shakespeare; I'm sick of all of it.

DES THE MOANER.

...You English and your tedious preoccupation with Shakespeare! Surely you don't have to be Russian and Irish like us to appreciate you have other great poets?

C. ZHANOV
MISS TZAND
MEL O'FRUITFULNESS.

...We would like to point out to the ladies who complained of the lack of Shakespearean contributions to Pseudo Names that we have been writing in from Venice for some time, without success. It's as if you regard us as somehow inferior.

F.U. PRICKUS
DWAYNE OTTBLEED
F.Y. POISONOUS
DWAYNE KNOTT-DYE.

...Shakespeare is over-rated. What about those other great renaissance playwrights, Ben Johnson and Christopher Marlowe?

VAL PONY
TAM BURR-LAYNE.

...I utterly deplore the axing of the Light Brigade in the latest defence spending review.

ARTHUR LEIGH GONWARD.

...Though I write as a chap, I cannot t ell you what joy and happiness the appearance of so many Shakespearean efforts in your popular "Pseudo Names" column has brought to the married womenfolk of our little Berkshire town.

MURRAY WIVES (of Windsor).

...We've been doing a bit of research, and it seems that not since the development of commedia dell'arte in 18th century Italy has European culture been so enriched as it has been with the introduction of your Pseudo Names section.

R. LE QUINN
N. COLUMBINE.

...The last two issues have been sadly lacking in Shakespearean pseudo names. Can we arrange a date when the two of us could meet the editor once again to discuss how we might raise the tone of this amusing feature?

WAYNE SHALWE III
MIA TAGEN.

...Anyone expecting to come up with new ideas at this stage is surely tilting at windmills...

DON K. HOTY.

...I have a theory about the deeper meaning of your Pseudo Names section and its physical and spiritual significance for humanity. Unfortunately I am not at liberty to reveal it to you.

ROSY KRUSHAN.

...Looking back through several recent copies of the Eye, I became enraged at the waste of space given to the nonsense that constitutes Pseudo Names. And you don't even bother to give the place where these so-called letter writers live!

LUKE BACKIN
Ongar.

...I think The King's Speech could be made into a great novel.

IKE LAUDIUS.

...In response to Rosy Kryshnan's Pseudo Names entry (issue 1283), I know the deeper meaning of Pseudo Names and am eager to share it. All **you** need to do is read L. Ron Hubbard.

DIANE ETTICKS.

...I had to give a funeral oration last week, and it went rather well.

PERRY CLEESE.

...With regard to Shakespearean Pseudo Names, we disagree with recent correspondents (Wayne Shalwee III, Mia Tagen), who are obviously scheming to their own secret agenda. This Tudor twaddle does not "raise the tone", so we urge the editor to show courage and do what must be done: kill this column immediately.

EVA TWERE-DUNNE
BETSY B. DUNNE-QUICKLY.

FIRST DRAFTS

AESOP

Jane Austen

Elizabeth Gilbert

Vladimir Nabokov

Emily Dickinson

OSAMA DEAD

Those Headlines In Full

WORLD WILL BE A SAFER PLACE

Top Level Worldwide Security Alert Declared

The Mailygraph
13 MAY 2011

WORLD EXCLUSIVE

HOW THE WORLD REACTED TO THE DEATH OF OSAMA BIN LADEN

President Obama: My fellow Americans. The long night is over. The dawn has broken. Darkness flees in the face of the eternal light. But there must be no triumphalism, no brandishing of the trophies of victory. Yes, we got him and Dubya didn't! Vote for me!! Geronimo!!!

Former President GW Bush: I am delighted that Obama is dead. I never liked the guy and it's not just cos he's a Muslim. And give those seals a fish from me!

The Mayor of London Boris Johnson: Crikey! Old Beardy has copped it, what? Well, good riddance say I, though we had better watch out for all the other fruitcakes coming out of the woodwork blowing up our bicycles!! Mind you, those photos of Osama's niece, eh? Phwoar!! Dingus dongus!! Hello!!

Lord Fellowes: The Bin Ladens were never quite top drawer in Saudi society, and the fact that Osama's father was in, horror of horrors, the construction industry, rather speaks for itself. I certainly would never have placed him next to a Duchess at dinner as he would probably have eaten his sheep's eyes with the wrong fork!!

Mohammed al Fayed: Forget the fuggin' seals! It was the Duke of Edinburgh who killed him driving a white Fiat helicopter into the compound in order to stop the Muslim Osama marrying fuggin' Pippa Middleton!!

"All right, have it your way – you heard a seal bark"

NB after Thurber

'I Go Inside The £1 Million Hideaway Of The World's Most Evil Man'

TODAY I saw with my own eyes the incredible 5-star luxury mansion in which the world's top terrorist leader secretly enjoyed a life of sybaritic self-indulgence with his many wives.

The palatial 8-bedroom home, which for five long years was the nerve centre of Al Qaeda, the sinister worldwide organisation responsible for literally millions of deaths, stands in the leafy suburb of Abbottabad, Pakistan's equivalent of Tunbridge Wells or Cheltenham Spa.

House Price Shock

Local estate agents told me that if put on the market now, Bin Laden's former home would fetch at least 3 trillion bhuttos, the equivalent of £1 million.

Yesterday I was the first British journalist to be allowed beyond the 30-foot concrete wall which hides Bin Laden's bolthole from the prying eyes of the world's security forces, where I saw for myself the amazing Arabian Nights-style luxury from which the world's most wanted criminal was happy to send his army of willing acolytes to their deaths, while they sipped cups of herbal tea, lolling on richly-woven carpets flown in from the souks of Waziristan.

When I went upstairs my eyes were literally dazzled by the shiny silver-plated taps on the mass-murderer's huge jacuzzi-style 3-foot long bath.

And in the sumptuous master bedroom where the evil genius behind 9/11 finally met his much-deserved end, not even the

*by **Lunchtime O'Bore***
Abbottabad, Tuesday

bloodstains on the floor could disguise the fact that, with a bit of renovation, the house could easily fetch an asking price of 2 trillion bhuttos, which would mark it out as very much one of the most desirable properties in this highly sought after residential district, close to Pakistan's top military academy with good transport links to all destinations, including the exclusive cave system of the nearby Bora Bora mountains.

Wheelie Bin Laden

Neighbours I spoke to yesterday were amazed to discover that the quietly-spoken bearded recluse they knew only as "Mr Bin Laden" had been mixed up in some of the world's worst terrorist atrocities.

Said one local IT specialist, Mr Gughal Fezbuck, "He was a bit of a loner, but he sometimes used to ask the local children to come in to watch videos of Postman Pat and young martyrs blowing themselves up.

"But he was not one to join in on the local barbecue circuit, or to join my wife's Reading-the-Koran-Group.

"The only really odd thing about him was that he never seemed to put out his rubbish bin like the rest of us, and he didn't for some reason seem to want to be on the telephone.

"I, more than once," said Mr Fezbukh, "tried to interest him in broadband, but he told me very politely that if I didn't go away, he would kill me. He was a very nice man with beautiful manners. We shall miss him."

THE LAST DAYS OF OSAMA

Viewers may find the following scenes disturbing

There's far too much violence on TV nowadays...

...and it's all repeats

PENTAGON CHANGES OSAMA STORY AGAIN

THE top US General in charge of the mission to apprehend the late Osama bin Laden has once again revised his account of the events surrounding his accidental execution.

He told journalists, "Contrary to earlier reports – many of them by myself – that Osama was hiding behind his wife and carrying an automatic weapon, I would now like to make it clear that Osama was in fact charging at Navy Seals, mounted on Shergar, whilst carrying Iraqi-made weapons of mass destruction and was using Lord Lucan as a human shield."

(Reuters)

How the job has changed him

President Obama

President Rambobama

Lines on the Award of a Knighthood to Mr Bruce Forsyth

BY WILLIAM REES-McGONAGALL

'Twas in the year of Two Thousand and Eleven
That at the advanced age of nearly eighty-seven
Mr Bruce Forsyth, after waiting so long,
Was finally informed he'd been given a gong.

For many a moon the nation had protested Brucie's right
To be dubbed by the Queen a very parfit, gentle knight.
"Arise Sir Brucie!" was what they wanted to hear
But they were disappointed year after year after year.

For who had deserved more to enter the nation's hall
　　　　　　　　　　of fame
Than the long-service compère of The Generation Game?
Not, since Marie Curie discovered radium,
Had there been such a triumph as Bruce in Sunday
　　　　　　　　Night at the London Palladium.

And who could be more worthy of becoming a knight
Than the brilliant presenter of Play Your Cards Right?
While even in old age he remained entrancing
As the twinkling host of Strictly Come Dancing.

But there was one thing above all for which Brucie
　　　　　　　　　　deserved special praise,
Namely his witty and truly unforgettable catchphrase
"Nice to see you, to see you nice".
The whole nation could repeat it, if asked, in a trice.

Old men in pubs, young girls on meeting,
They all could repeat his celebrated greeting.
And each time they said it, they chortled anew
"To see you nice, nice to see you."

And for this truly amazing feat
Only one honour was apt and meet.
A visit to the Palace, a tap with a sword,
That was to be Sir Brucie's fitting reward.

"Have you come far?" Her Majesty would say,
And all the crowd would shout "Hooray!".
"Nice to see you," she might conceivably add.
"To see you nice," would be the answer to make all
　　　　　　　　　　her subjects glad.

© W. Rees-McGonagall

"Why can't we just visit your mother on her website?"

A Message from the London Mayor

What ho chaps. Boris here. Just reminding you what a first-class job I'm making of running dear old London. I'm even forking out for my own Olympic tickets to save you chaps money on freebies. Pretty impressive, what? I wish I could say the same for my old friend in Downing Street. I don't want to be disloyal to a fellow OE, but sometimes you have to speak your mind to a chum who's making a bit of a balls of things. Don't get me wrong. Cammers is a nice enough chap, and was savvy enough to pick a very fruity wife with a fair bit of moolah attached. But the fact is that those of us who were scholars back at Slough Comp always knew that Dave was not exactly a brain box. Jolly smooth and all that but, frankly, a couple of light bulbs short of a chandelier, if you take my meaning. No disrespect to Dave who I'm sure is doing his best, but he's made a pretty good dog's breakfast of everything to date, viz, hospitals, Libya, forests, transport, cuts, housing, immigration, wife not wearing a hat at the Royal Wedding. I mean it's all a bit of a pig's ear, isn't it. Chum Cameron, let's face it, has made more U-turns than a cabbie on Oxford Street trying to knock down an innocent cyclist like yours truly. So what's to be done? I'm not saying that Calamity Cameron should throw in the towel straight away. But I would just like everyone to know that when that day comes (and it may come sooner than he thinks!), there is someone standing by, full of beans and bottle, and with experience of running one of the world's major cities, who's popular with the Tory rank and file and can rally the troops, who is only too ready to help out in getting the whole show back on the road. And by the way, I haven't even mentioned that fatuous Big Society idea which was an obvious non-starter if ever I saw one. Talk about a pyramid of piffle! Still good luck to Dave in the stormy days ahead. I'm right behind him. Just like Brother Brutus in the play. Et tu Boris, what!

Bojo, London Mayor

"Working towards a future in Downing Street"

"I try to keep the room just as it was the day he died"

COURT CIRCULAR

That Obama State Procession

1st Bullet Proof Car

President Obama; HM The Queen.

1st Helicopter Hovering Ahead

42 members of the US Navy Seals led by Lieutenant Kurt Asskicker III Junior.

2nd Bullet Proof Car

First Lady Michele Obama; HRH The Duke of Edinburgh; Inspector Kevin Knacker of the Elite Royal Protection Squad.

2nd Helicopter

Crashed in Trafalgar Square

3rd Bullet Proof Car

The Rt Hon David Cameron; Not Nick Clegg; Ms Hillary Clintstone (subject to availability).

1st Bicycle

Boris Johnson, Mayor of London.

2nd Bicycle

Steve Hilton, Big Soc Adviser to PM.

1st Car Speeding Past Procession

Chris Huhne (or possibly Mrs Huhne).

(That's enough procession, Ed.)

THAT MILITARY COVENANT ENSHRINED IN LAW IN FULL

THE Government will treat those soldiers risking their life for this country with the utmost dignity and respect.

We will achieve this by closing down armed forces rehab centres for injured service personnel and slashing rehab and counselling services for those suffering from mental health issues in line with budget cuts elsewhere.

We will ensure that servicemen sleeping rough on the streets have free blankets and a hot meal provided by a charity which has been forced to do the work because cash-strapped councils are no longer able to provide such services.

We'll wear a poppy on Armistice Day and a sad face.

Er...

That's it.

WORLD FAILS TO END
— Loony goes into hiding

by Our Rapture Staff
Jeremiah Clarkson

A SOMERSET prophet who predicted that the world would end on the 21st May was said to be disappointed today when his prophecy failed to be fulfilled.

Lord Rees Mogg, 97, known as Mystic Mog to his followers (Sid and Doris Bonkers-Smythe) was said to be "in hiding" in his library listening to his Sony Walkman and refusing to take calls from the media.

Mogg had worked out the exact date of the end of the world using a complicated formula involving the gold standard, the rate of inflation, global warming and the number of first class degrees awarded to members of the cabinet.

When "the Rapture" failed to materialise shortly after the six o'clock news on Saturday, Rees-Mogg (continued p94)

Those Schwarzenegger Catchphrases In Full

I'll be back... when my wife's out shopping

Hasta la vista, Arnie's baby!

I won't be back

MING MING – WORLD'S OLDEST LIB DEM NOT DEAD

by Our Zoological Staff
LUNCHTIME O'ZOOZE and APANDA PLATELL

NATURE lovers were delighted last night at the news that the world's oldest, Chinese-Scottish Lib Dem ex-leader is not dead, despite reports to the contrary.

In fact, say his keepers, Ming Ming is showing all the signs of renewed life, and could be well placed to return to the leadership of the Lib Dem party, following the

disgrace of his fellow pandas, Clegg Clegg, Huhne Huhne and Law Laws.

Ming Ming is 106.

POLLY FILLER

AM I the only one who is heartily sick of Pippa Middleton's derrière? No? Thought not. There must be millions of us hard-working mums who are fed up with their useless partners watching re-runs of the Royal Wedding on Sky Plus Anytime HD with the screen paused on the moment Miss P. bends down to rearrange Kate's bridal train!

Apart from the fact that she is twenty years younger than you, Simon, I don't suppose she goes for the middle-aged, overweight, balding type who spills wine down his shirt whilst falling asleep watching Jeremy Clarkson's Extreme Injunctions on Dave Legal Plus One!

In fact, she is so out of your league it's like toddler Charlie's Under 8s 'B' team from The Toby Young Free Pre-School For The Differently Middle Class taking on Manchester United... that's how tragic you are, Simon.

...Sorry, where was I? Oh yes, the idea that going to a couple of Pilates classes can give you the bottom that launched a thousand websites is about as ludicrous as the idea that Pippa would give a second glance to the paunchy man who put his microwave curry for one in the tumble dryer on the one occasion that the stupid au pair had a day off to attend her parents' funeral in Benghazi...

Where was I? Oh yes, let's face it, Pippa dear, we don't all have time to go to posh exercise classes all day. Some of us have jobs to do and children to look after – including the flabby, middle-aged child on the sofa who is following Jemima Khan on Twitter, who incidentally is another one with whom you would be punching way above your weight – and that is some weight, let's face it.

THE TRUTH is that us do-it-all working mums don't need fancy work-outs and personal trainers to stay in trim – we get all the exercise we need by juggling our career and family commitments on the tightrope of modern life!

And the result? Only last week I climbed out of a taxi and a fan who had read one of my columns shouted "Polly Filler! What an arse!" You see? Eat your heart out, Pips – it doesn't get better than that!

© Polly Filler 2011.

NEW DEMANDS FOR GAGAING ORDER

by Our Legal Staff **Phil Courts**

THERE were growing demands yesterday for the issue of a so-called "Gagaing order" on the publicity-seeking celebrity known only as Lady Gaga.

This superstar injunction would require the singer and performance artist to "shut up for a bit" and "disappear from the pages of all newspapers" until further notice.

Freedom of speechless

"This is a matter of genuine public interest," claimed a lawyer acting for the nation. "The public has a right to know a lot less about Lady Gaga and we certainly don't need to see intimate photos of her with no clothes on or wearing one of her stupid outfits made out of meat."

Poker faceless

The lawyer continued, "Any Gagaing order would require her image to be blacked out and her voice to be muted, otherwise parents of children all over Britain will be sent crying home from school with bloody Lady Gaga blaring out on the car stereo again *(That's enough, Ed.)*

I did not come into journalism to go around shagging journalists

Surely "gagging" journalists...

First pictures of child Andrew Marr wrongly thought was his

"I thought we were through with all these super injunctions"

GLENDA SLAGG
The First Lady of Tweet Street!?! Geddit?!!?!!?

■ HATS off to Princess Beatrice! She's the Feisty Ferglet whose not afraid to wear a fun fashionable fascinator and then sell it off for chariddee?!!!? Which goes to prove that she's got a heart of pure gold!!? Take a tip from your gorgeous granddaughter Queenie and put your crown on e-bay to raise money for the victims of the Irish Potato famine!!?? (Geddit?!!)

■ PRINCESS Beatrice?!! Call that a hat?! It looked like a toilet seat to me darling which is where it deserved to be flushed?!!?! (Geddit??!) No wonder the Queen looked embarrassed on Wills' Big Day – come on yer Maj, off with Bea's head and then she won't be able to wear any more stupid hats?!?!

■ THREE cheers for Mrs Huhne, that's Vicky Price to you Mister Pressman?!! Every woman in the country is right behind you Vicky for getting your own back on yer cheating hubby as he drives around the M11 a honkin' and a bonkin'?!? Hell hath no fury, as the Poet says, like a woman forced to take her love-rat's points?!?! You put your foot down Vicky, just like Criminal Chris did – and now he's on a one way street to Jail!?! And serve him right!?!

■ Put a sock in it Vicky love!?! You're making a fool of yourself – looking like a Harpy from Hell going after poor hubby Huhne for some trivial offence that took place years ago!!!? No wonder he was driving so fast?!!? Anything to get away from you?!??! (Geddit?!!?!!) And guess what love you've **driven** him into the arms of beautiful bisexual Cutie-Pie Carina Trimingham the dishy dyke from the Dept of Energy (Geddit?!!???)

■ Read Jeffrey Archer's new book?!?? Me neither?!!! Here's a *novel* idea from Auntie Glenda: – send him back to prison!!! No offence Jeff?!!?!! Although you did commit one!!!? Remember??!!

■ HERE THEY ARE – Glenda's Flower Show Fancies:

● Dominique Strauss-Kahn – He's the Head of the World Bank!!!! Ok so he's a compulsive rapist!?!! Who isn't these days??!!!??

● Ken Clarke – Ok so he's old, fat and out of touch on rape!!?? Who isn't these days???!?!

● Arnie Schwarzenegger – They call him the Terminator?!?! Fornicator more like?!! Still at least he's not a rapist?!! At the time of going to press, anyway?!!?!!?!

Byeee!!

SABINE WOMEN SHOCK

Is this your first IMF conference?

IMF✱✱✱ED

THAT DSK AMERICAN-FRENCH DICTIONARY IN FULL

No *adv.* Oui.

WHO SHOULD RUN THE IMF?

YOU choose the safe pair of hands to sort out the World's economy.

❶ Arnold Schwarzenegger
❷ Silvio Berlusconi
❸ Bill Clinton
❹ Sir Fred Goodwin
❺ Charlie Sheen
❻ Ken Clarke
❼ Gordon Brown

(That's enough candidates. Ed)

MADDIE LATEST
KNACKER TO JOIN HUNT FOR PUBLICITY

by Our Crime Staff **R Guido**

ON THE direct orders of prime minister David Cameron, Inspector 'Knacker of the Yard' Knacker has set up a dedicated 30-strong team of detectives to win favourable media coverage for Mr Cameron by investigating the mystery of the missing four-year-old Madeleine McCann.

Said the Inspector last night, "We expect to spend a considerable amount of time in Portugal, taking full cognizance of the local circumstances relating to this unfortunate case, ie enjoying the sea, sunshine and fine local wines."

He continued, "The past few years have been every policeman's nightmare. We have been continually accused of killing innocent people, accusing blameless schoolmasters of murder and failing to arrest Mr Murdoch for phone tapping."

"But now at last we have the chance to recover our lost reputation which has been missing for so long."

I ♡ LIB DEMS

HOW'S MY WIFE'S DRIVING?

LAWS — 'I Should Not Have Lived A Lie'

by our Political staff **Matthew Gay Parris**

FORMER cabinet minister David Laws has issued a statement of regret over his recent fall from grace. He told reporters, "I should not have hidden my criminality. It was a mistake to think it would never come out. Now I have admitted that I am a practising criminal I feel much better about myself."

He went on, "It was of course a complete surprise to my parents. They thought I was straight, but now they know that I am bent.

However, they have been very good and accepted it and I now wish I had been honest about my criminality years ago."

Second Home-o-Sexual

Mr Laws hopes that by going public in this way, he will prove a role model to younger crooks who are often confused about their true nature and try to keep it secret. *(We get the idea. Ed.)*

"Lib Dems, they're all beards and scandals!"

The Eye's Controversial New Columnist

He shares his thoughts with the nation so his mind can be rid of them

What is the problem with Nick Clegg??? The poor man hasn't a clue. He blubs away and then asks to be left alone! Any baby will tell you, one cries FOR attention, not for LACK of attention! Speaking as a baby *(see photo)* I cry when I'm hungry or when I've done dirties in my nappy. Mr Clegg should only bawl when he's messed his pants. Keep your powder dry, Mr Clegg, until after the by-elections. Then you can *(cont. p. 94)*

DESPERATE BUSINESS

JON & MICK / MODERN TOSS

and I see you went to Cambridge

yeah I had to drop something off for someone, I was back by half six

How would you feel about reapplying for your job?

I didn't want it in the first place

say what you like about his sales technique but he shifts a lot of fridges

yeah ok I'll take it

hello I'm the new mobile library service, do you want to borrow our book?

I WAS GLAD

by Dame Sylvie Krin, author of *La Dame Aux Camillas,
The Heir of Sorrows, etc*

THE STORY SO FAR: Charles has been invited by the BBC to make a historic documentary about his favourite composer, Sir Hubert Parry. Now read on...

"THE thing about Parry is that he was so marvellously English. He represented the essence of the whole English thingie..."

"Cut!" Sir Alain de Botney, the BBC's legendary director of arts documentaries, interrupted the Prince of Wales in the middle of his piece to camera.

"That's absolutely marvellous, Your Royal Highness, but I wonder if we could try it once more, losing the word 'thingie', which I don't think was in the script we gave you this morning."

It was Take 32, and Charles was beginning to get slightly peeved by the constant interruptions from his director.

"I was just trying to inject a note of informality to liven it up. Otherwise people might think it was a bit, you know, boring."

At the back of the set the 89 members of the BBC Philanthropic Orchestra waited patiently for their cue to begin playing Parry's most famous tune, *Jerusalem*.

The twelve-person film crew with equal patience reset their cameras for Take 33.

Sir Alain diplomatically suggested a solution to their temporary impasse.

"Perhaps, sire, we could move on to the bit where you read out the letter, and return to the bit about Englishness later on?"

Charles readily assented. "Yes, I'm looking forward to this bit. It's really incredibly moving."

"Quiet, please," ordered Sir Alain.

The set was hushed, broken only by a stifled yawn from the second trombonist.

Charles was then handed a yellowing document by the curator of the Parry Archive in Merioneth.

Turning to the camera, he began to speak from the heart.

"You see, it's a very sad story. Parry was a brilliantly talented man in all sorts of ways, not just music. And then he married this much younger girl from a very aristocratic family.

"But the tragic thing is that she never really appreciated his gifts and showed no interest in all the things that really mattered to him."

There was a hint of a catch in Charles' voice, as his deepest emotions almost overcame him. A tear welled up in his eye. "Architecture, the environment, holistic medicine, the Book of Common Prayer... She cared nothing about all these hugely important issues of the time, but just sat around listening to her Walkman..."

"Cut! That's tremendous stuff, sire," broke in Sir Alain. "But I think that we may again be wandering a little from the script. I wonder if we should have a short break here.

"Why don't you take a seat, sire, while we run through some of the music."

"Good idea," agreed Charles, as a large, ornate, velvet-covered chair was carried in by a team from the BBC props department, who had made it specially for the occasion.

"I hope you're going to play that passage I particularly asked for from the great man's 15th Symphony. I think they called it *The Interminable*, although I gather it hasn't been played for over 100 years. Astonishing, considering that it must be one of the finest symphonies ever written."

"Quite, sire, we're really hoping to find room for that. But we thought for now we'd start with the Coronation anthem, *I Was Glad.*"

The musicians began to tune up as the 90-strong singers of the Schola Cambrensis, BBC Wales's Devolved Choral Ensemble, stood up and prepared to sing.

Charles settled back into his velvet "throne". He felt relaxed, as the music swelled around him...

THE music was swelling around him as Charles stood at the door of Westminster Abbey.

The great day for which he had been waiting so long had come at last.

Before him a vast congregation of dignitaries and notables from Britain and all over the world turned expectantly to the Great West Door.

He could see President Obama, the Crown Prince Shufti al Bakhanda of Qatar and the exiled King Nicholas of Bulgaria. And wasn't that Sir Elton John with his partner, Lady Gaga, and their baby, Montezuma?

And in the distance, holding the crown aloft, ready to place it on the head of the new King, a venerable trio of bearded prelates, representing all the faiths: the Archbishop of Canterbury, the Chief Rabbi and the Chief Imam of Finsbury Park Mosque.

And suddenly, the mighty organ began to thunder out the familiar strains of Parry's immortal *I Was Glad*, the anthem which since time immemorial had signalled the arrival of the monarch to be crowned King.

This, Charles knew in the deepest fibres of his being, was the supreme moment of his life.

"Excuse me, sir, could you please sit down?" said a verger who had taken the Prince's arm.

"King William and Queen Kate are just arriving now – we've put you behind the Middletons."

The pure voices of the choir blazed forth in an exultant blast of joyful sound.

"I was glad..."

"No, no," thought Charles. "I'm not at all glad. There's been a terrible mistake. It really is appalling," he shouted.

CHARLES woke with a shudder. "Are you alright, sire?" Sir Alain was looking down at him with a look of deepest concern on his bearded face.

"Yes, I'm absolutely fine. I must have nodded off or something," replied Charles.

"Very good, sire," soothed Sir Alain, as he turned back to the now silent array of musicians, singers, cameramen, lighting operators and members of the BBC's much-feared health and safety compliance directorate.

"Sorry, everyone," he said. "I'm afraid we're going to have to record the whole thing again. Some idiot was shouting backstage. And I'm awfully sorry, sire," he added, turning back to the seated Prince, "but that means we won't have time for your symphony. Perhaps we could put it in another programme."

Charles felt a familiar wave of disappointment sweep over him. Why was it that really great men were never appreciated in their own time...?

(To be continued)

© *Dame Sylvie Krin, winner of the 2011 Ryanair Romantic Airport Fiction Prize for her recent runaway bestseller "Where There's A Wills There's A Kate".*

GNOME CROSS CARE HOMES
A Statement

IT IS with great regret that I must announce the impending bankruptcy of Gnome Cross Care Homes, the world renowned retirement-to-grave conglomerate with over 7,500 registered homes in the Eastbourne region alone.

The accusation that we at Gnome Cross do not care about the elderly is as hurtful as it is demonstrably untrue.

Our concern at Gnome Cross has always been to provide the maximum comfort to those in the twilight of their lives.

Take the example of Lord G., an elderly private equity billionaire who, thanks to Gnome Cross, is able to live in conditions of extreme luxury in many homes throughout the world, including Barbados, attended by expert nurses and trained masseuses to cater for all his needs. Indeed, Lord G. has a lump sum provision of over £28 million set aside by Gnome Cross – just for his care alone.

Critics of Gnome Cross would do well to bear these facts in mind before they make ill-informed judgements about companies who make obscene profits whilst being indifferent to the plight of senior citizens and who expect the taxpayer to foot the bill when they go belly up.

Lord Gnome

Gnome Cross Homes *We Care – You Pay!!*

CARE QUALITY COMMISSION DEFENDS INSPECTION OF HOMES

By **Simon Hogarth**

THE CARE Quality Commission has defended its system of inspections of care homes in the wake of the Winterborne View abuse scandal, whilst admitting it does have a slight backlog.

"We have just finished compiling the paperwork for our inspection of Bedlam which we visited on June 9 1735 and which we found to be an excellent facility, employing the very latest medical treatment for troubled patients, including ice baths and lobotomies," said a CQC spokesman. "We were particularly impressed by the 'meet an inmate' open days where members of the public were invited in to taunt and laugh at the patients.

"We would suggest the patients abused at Winterbourne be transferred to a 5* rated facility such as Bedlam to enjoy the very best care."

"You've never really embraced consumer culture, have you?"

That Irish Banquet for the Queen
Menu in Full

Potato Soup

– ❧ –

Baked Potato with Mash Chips

Potatoes Dauphinoise

Sautéed Potatoes

– ❧ –

Potato Ice Cream

– ❧ –

Petit Potatoes

– ❧ –

To drink:

Potcheen 1846

"Well, I think the Queen's trying really hard..."

THE MAILY TELEGRAPH | FRIDAY, JUNE 24 2011

Notebook
BRYONY GORMLESS

There's a lot about Take That in the papers. I love Take That and I always have done. Lots of my best friends didn't use to like the band at all but now they do. That's certainly worth writing about.

☐ Guess what! I saw Pippa Middleton's bottom in the paper the other day. And you know what? I can't think of anything interesting to say about it. Isn't that interesting?

☐ I read a pointless survey about something in the paper the other day. How pointless is that? The only thing more pointless would be if someone wrote a piece about it in the paper. Now that would be pointless!

☐ I've just read in the paper the three paragraphs I have just written. Why on earth are they there? Whatever next? Another paragraph?

Lookalikes

Rebekah   **Gorgon**

Sir,

Has anybody else noticed the remarkable similarity between Rebekah Brooks, ex-chief executive of News International and the Gorgons, who had serpents for hair, and were so frightful that their glance turned their victims to stone? Is Ms Brooks by any chance descended from one of these ladies, and if so, which one is it? Medusa was mortal, but the other two weren't.

Yours sincerely,
LOUISE GRAHAME,

York.

Fry   **Rutherford**

Sir,

Is it my imagination or is Stephen Fry slowly maturing into Dame Margaret Rutherford?
National treasures, the pair of 'em.
TOM ROONEY,

Dublin.

Gollum   **Rompuy**

Sir,

It has come to my attention that one of the gnomes of Brussels bears a remarkable resemblance to a famous hobbit. Do you think they might, perchance, be related?
Yours,
ROBERT BANKER,

Via email.

John   **Julian**

Sir,

What do Julian Assange and John Inman have in common? "I'm free..."
ISABEL FORBES,

Flintshire.

Diderot   **Cameron**

Sir,

Isn't the fact that David Cameron is the 295-year-old French Philosophe and Encyclopédiste Denis Diderot rather concerning?
ANDREW TICKELL,

Via email.

Kid Rock   **Mark Kennedy**

Sir,

Recently the Crown Prosecution Service has come under fire for embedding Mark Kennedy into the environmental movement as an agent provocateur. This claim is absurd considering Mark Kennedy was already embedded in America as Pamela Anderson's husband and country rocker "Kid Rock".
FREDERICK GHAHRAMANI,

Vancouver.

Banana Split   **Carr**

Sir,

I would be interested to learn from any of your readers, what became of the other three Banana Splits?
PHILLIP SMITH,

Portsmouth.

Micky   **Vicky**

Sir,

Any chance that Vicky Huhne is Mick Jagger reincarnated? Oops sorry, I forgot he's still alive...
Yours eternally,
JOHN MOWER,

Brighton.

Cooper   **Winkleman**

Sir,

Did you notice that when Claudia and Alice appeared on Strictly Come Dancing, they were never seen together? Is there something we should know?
Regards,
JULIAN WATSON,

Selby.

Peston   **Lowry**

Sir,

I was struck the other day by the remarkable resemblance of LS Lowry and Robert Peston. One paints bleak pictures of the northern industrial landscape and the other was a famous artist from Lancashire. Are they related by any chance?
JIM HERBERT,

Via email.

Marina   **Cher**

Sir,

Has anyone noticed the difference between X Factor hopeful Cher Lloyd and Marina from Stingray? Of course, we can but only hope that Cher gains the vocal range of Marina.
NEIL FAULKNER,

Via email.

Masterchef   **Neanderthal**

Sir,

I was fascinated to learn from a BBC headline that scientists have discovered that Neanderthals cooked and ate vegetables.
Perhaps this is not surprising since our antecedents appear to resemble uncannily the modern hunter-gatherer, self sufficiency guru and Masterchef contestant, Dick Strawbridge.
DR BARRY WIBOURN,

Rayleigh, Essex.

Austin Powers   **Anne Robinson**

Sir,

I couldn't help noticing that, according to the Daily Telegraph, Austin Powers has appeared at the Hay Festival. However, on second look I realised it was in fact his mother.

Yeah Baby, etc,
NICHOLAS HAYLAND,

Via email.

Meatloaf   **Balls**

Sir,

It is back a few weeks now, but when Meat Loaf appeared on Andrew Neil's This Week programme, I came into the room and thought that Ed Balls had gone casual.

LESLIE HARGREAVES,

Via email.

Crisp   **Crisper**

Sir,

Did Dame Maggie Smith take inspiration for her raved-over performance in Downton Abbey from the original stately homo of England?

MICHAEL EWART,

Via email.

Wally   **Rees-Mogg**

Sir,

Your profile of the new boy Jacob Rees-Mogg and other recent coverage is incomplete. You speak of his sister Anunziata and of his father Lord Rees-Mogg, and omit the rest of the family. I have begun to wonder if Jacob did in fact have a twin brother from whom he was separated at birth. I suggest this brother may have originally been named Walsingham, but in accordance with Dave's policy this name has now been shortened to Wally.

ENA COWPAT,

Deepest Somerset.

Georgey   **Chucky**

Sir,

I wonder if any of your readers have noticed an uncanny resemblance between the Chancellor of the Exchequer, George Osborne, and Chucky in Child's Play? Certainly both appear most proficient slashers!

Yours faithfully,
TOM BROWN,

London SW5.

Actress   **Fiancée**

Sir,

Have others noticed the striking similarity between royal fiancée, Kate Middleton, and the actress Martine McCutcheon?

In the film 'Love Actually' Miss McCutcheon implausibly plays an ordinary, pretty girl who manages to court, and finally catch, one of the most important men in the land.

What romantic twaddle!

Yours,
LYNNE BOOTH,

Via email.

Pop star   **Pop star**

Sir,

Is Professor Brian Cox the love child of Aerosmith's Steve Tyler? He seems to have inherited his pop star talent from someone?

Cheers,
DAVID SCHOFIELD,

Via email.

Blatter   **Fayed**

Sir,

These denialists all look the same to me. One old fugger. Another old fugger?

Yours truly,
LIONEL PRODGERS,

London, SE19.

Simple Primate   **Ape**

Sir,

Has anyone noticed, as I have, the extraordinary similarity between the Ambam, the gorilla who walks like a man, and Andy Gray, the former commentator on Sky Sports? Are they by any chance related?

ENA B. SKY-BEE,

Via email.

Wendolene   **Karen**

Sir,

Has anyone noticed the similarity between Karen Buck the Labour spokeswoman on work and pensions and Wendolene an inanimate plasticine model from "Wallace and Gromit"?

KEITH KENNEDY,

Switzerland.

Pickles   **Clown**

Sir,

The chief executive of Barnsley council branded secretary of state for communities and local government a "clown" for saying that local government cuts would not effect well-run councils. Does Mr Pickles inherit this unusual outlook from a proud family tradition?

LIZ MCKINNLELL,

Via email.

Rebekah   **Mick**

Sir,

While staff at The News of the World may find out that "Money's too Tight to Mention" in forthcoming months, they may take up some of their new-found time to contemplate the uncanny resemblance between Rebekah Brooks and Mick Hucknall, the flame-haired crooner from Simply Red. Another coincidence is, of course, the News of the World is simply not read anymore....

JONATHAN SMITH,

Via email.

SPOT THE BUNG COMPETITION!

Put your X where **you** think the bung is!

Clue: There may be more than one bung – or even 186 of them!

Send your completed Spot-the-Bung entry to Sepp Blatter, c/o Fifa, in a brown envelope including $100,000 in cash or you won't win.

OUTRAGE OVER CORRUPT ELECTION

By Our Football Staff **Fifa Glover**

THERE was widespread international condemnation of the Fifa Presidential election last night when it emerged that Sepp Blatter had triumphed over nobody to win football's top job by a margin of 186 to 17.

Said one critic, a Mr R. Mugabe of Zimbabwe, "This makes a mockery of the democratic process. It is totally unbelievable."

I Can't Believe It's Not Blatter

Another observer, a Mr Kim Jong-Il of North Korea, commented, "Sepp Blatter is giving fraudulent, unopposed dictatorship a bad name. He should be ashamed of himself."

However, some electoral experts were less keen to criticise the Fifa results. Said Nick Clegg, "Under AV, Mr Blatter would have still won, but it would have been fairer."

Mr Blatter celebrated his victory by announcing that the winners of the 2022 World Cup would be Qatar, who "will defeat France in the Semis and then win 3-2 in a close final with Argentina".

Getting Through To The Pay-Offs

Meanwhile, Fifa sponsors Nike have expressed concern that the ongoing corruption allegations surrounding Fifa could affect their reputation.

"We've worked very hard over the years to establish ourselves as the benchmark for an unpleasant, ruthless corporation driven only by profit and the thought that, almost overnight, Fifa can just waltz in and establish itself as being far more despicable makes us *(cont. p. 94)*

Late News
● *Mars to host 2026 World Cup. "Conditions perfect for football" says Blatter.*

The Old Bakery

WE SELL ONLY GENUINE CORNISH PASTIES BAKED IN CORNWALL BY POLISH MIGRANT WORKERS

MILIBAND – 'MAGGIE MY HERO' SHOCK

By Our Political Staff **Polly Tory**

THE leader of the Labour Party, Mr Ed Miliband, has attempted to "reach out" beyond the traditional voters to supporters of other parties.

He is keen to attract not just disillusioned centrists, but also those on the right of the political spectrum.

Miliband has let it be known that not only does he intensely admire Mrs Thatcher, but regards the late Enoch Powell as "an inspiration to us all". He called him "an ardent moderniser, a conviction politician and a supreme patriot".

The Labour leader also cited as role models Mr Nick Griffin ("Radical"), Attila the Hun ("Visionary") and Genghis Khan ("Many good points").

However, he failed to endorse Labour colleagues, singling out one particular example as "a shifty, disloyal, untrustworthy troublemaker and sibling".

A spokesman for Mr David Miliband said later, "David has no idea who his brother is referring to, but then no one understands anything his brother says anyway, which is why David is 100 percent behind him".

There's no such thing as socialism

Now on stage! *Opening and closing soon*

SHRED THE MUSICAL

Hated ogre, Fred the Shred, has fallen in love with gorgeous senior colleague Princess VDM. But now a band of marauding hacks seek to reveal the identity of Shred's secret love. The romantic monster rushes to the courts to save his beloved from the baying mob. Will he succeed? Or will the Law prove itself a talking ass??

SONGS INCLUDE ★ ★
Banks for the Memory!
Scotland the Bust! ★
We're in the Papers!
Summertime and the Living is Eady!
(That's enough songs)

CAST IN FULL
● **Shred** Mr Fred Goodwin

● **Ass** Justice Eady

● **Princess VDM** (Name withheld for legal reasons)

● WARNING: Investors in Shred the Musical may lose all their money

Daily Mail

FRIDAY, JUNE 10, 2011

WILL DEADLY CUCUMBERS CAUSE FALL IN HOUSE PRICES?

By Our Science Editor **Phil Space**

ESTIMATES today, conjured up by made-up Daily Mail scientists, suggest that the current European E. coli outbreak, possibly linked to vegetables but probably not linked to cucumbers, will cost the lives of millions of unsuspecting Brits.

"We now expect that these killer vegetables will quickly mutate and then go on an indiscriminate killing spree, rampaging through British towns and cities eating everything in their path. Like in that film," said a man wearing his favourite white coat.

"This will be especially bad news for already hard-pressed homeowners already reeling as a result of the credit crunch, who as a direct result of the impending vegetable apocalypse crunch will see the value of their homes fall by as much as 700 or 800%.".

> **Will Contaminated Vegetables Spreading Deadly E. Coli Through Europe Eventually Kill Every Last One Of Us?**
> No.

OI, YOU SPILT MY PINT!

GOSH, THAT ESCALATED QUICKLY

APACHE

ROBERT THOMPSON

CHARLES MOORE'S NOTEBOOK

One of the most obvious signs of the decline of our once-great country is the impossibility of purchasing a perfectly ordinary silk top hat for everyday use. There was a time when silk top hat shops were to be found in every high street in the land. But alas, those days are long gone. Only last week I visited my local Tesco and asked the girl behind the till where silk top hats were to be found. She stared at me with blank incomprehension and suggested I might find something in Children's Party Hats on Aisle 23, next to flavoured yoghurts, whatever they might be. The story was the same in every shop I tried, including W.H. Smith, Poundstretcher and Kentucky Fried Chicken. I am no businessman, but it appears to me that there is a vast commercial opportunity here for one of our bright young entrepreneurs to make his fortune. Or are we no longer interested in reversing the decline of our once-envied manufacturing industries? Mr Cable, please note.
Reprinted without permission from the Spectacularlyboring.

TOP FOOTBALLER IN SEX SCANDAL NAMED

GLENDA SLAGG
Fleet Street's Deadly Cucumber!

■ WAYNE ROONEY!! Who do you think you're trying to kid, baldy!? All that money just to TRANSFER some flimsy follicles onto your thick skull!! Hair's the truth, Waynee – you looked like a spud before, now you look like a spud with hair!?!! Geddit??!!

■ HATS OFF to Wayne Rooney and take your hat off too, Wayne, so that we can all see your bouncy new barnet!?!! Hair's the truth Waynee – all the galls are a-dribblin' and a-droolin' for the new-look spud-faced nipper mark 2!! On me head son?!?!! Geddit??!

■ WOOR!!! Cheryl!! That's cool to you bonny lass!! *(Is this right? Ed.)* How dare those ignorant yanks dump our national treasure just because they can't understand a word she says!!? Shame on you Uncle so-called Sam?! Gizza job to woor Cheryl noo like!!? *(Are you sure this is right,? Ed.)*

■ SO CHERYL has been fired because the yanks couldn't understand her!?? Well no one over here has had a clue what she's been saying for years!! And even if they could, it wasn't worth listening to!!?! Take some advice from Auntie Glenda, Cheryl, now you've got the Axe Factor, petal, go back to Toonland and join all the other Geordies on the dool?!! Geddit!?!! *(This can't be right, Ed.)*

● Good old Giggsy!?! Glad to see the super-injunction worked so well!!?! Now we know about you, your sister-in-law, your brother and your auntie *(No, this time you're fired, Ed.)*

■ OK, HERE THEY ARE – Glenda's summertime sizzlers?!?!

● **Sir Vidia Naipaul!?!!** OK, so he thinks women can't write! There's plenty of other things we **can** do, Big Boy, just give us a call and we'll make Hay together!!?!

● **Sepp Blatter!?!!** Fifa's Mr Bung! How much to arrange a match round at my place?!? I suppose a 'fix' is out of the question?!!?

● **Tharanga Paranavitana** Crazy name, crazy opening batsman!?!!

Byeee!!

GIGGS IN SISTER-IN-LAW SHOCK

I told you I was a family man

ASSISTED SUICIDE TO BE SHOWN LIVE ON TV

By Our Dignity Staff **Hugh L. Thanasia**

A LEADING Cabinet minister will be shown by the BBC dying a slow painful death over the next two weeks.

The cameras will follow the 73-year old Andrew Lansley as he goes through the terminal stages of being sacked from his job.

Said a close friend and colleague, "Andrew has nothing left to live for. He has suffered enough. He doesn't want to be a burden to anybody, particularly his partner Dave.

"His only wish is that he be allowed to go with dignity."

But critics are unhappy about Mr Lansley's decision to commit political suicide, saying that it might encourage many of his colleagues to follow suit.

"If every one of us who's done a U-turn decides to end it all," said the critic, "there would be no one left in the Cabinet."

Kenneth Clarke is 107.

Forthcoming BBC Highlights

Top Yourself Gear Jeremy and the gang drive the latest 4x4s – off Beachy Head.

Suicide Watch Kate Humble and Chris Packham with more footage of lemmings.

Sir Terry and June June comes home to find Terry has topped himself... again!

Gardener's Goodbye Cruel World Carol and Monty plant hemlock, laburnum and deadly nightshade.

Also

● **Gas in the Attic** ● **Have I Got Noose For You** ● **Teletubbies** Time for Tubby Bye-Byes – for ever! ● **The Vulture Show** Novelist Sir Terry Pratchett explores the work of Sylvia Plath, Ernest Hemingway, Gertrude Bell, Virginia Woolf, Thomas Chatterton and others. *(Last in series.)*

"Excuse me, is this assisted suicide or have you just forgotten about me?"

KATE MOSS
How the years have taken their toll

1991

2011

THE TIMONS OF ATHENS
— Friday June 24 2011 —

Crisis Threat To Tourism

By Our Financial Staff
Harry Stophanes

London, Thursday

Thousands of public sector workers took to the streets of Britain yesterday to protest against the savage cuts to their pensions.

Four Horsemen of the Acropolis

As anger swept the streets, Greek holidaymakers have been warned to stay at home to avoid the strikes and the expected breakdown in law and order, thus depriving Britain of its only remaining industry – tourism.

Britain, which sees itself as a cradle of democracy, is now heading towards anarchy, with both its government and its banks collapsing and its population mutinous.

ON OTHER PAGES Bring Back the Drachma writes Christoferos Bookerides **2** Your Rains Tonight – Delphic Oracle in full **94** Can Our Boy Phillip (90) Rescue Britain **3**

"That's not for a holiday, that buys you Greece!"

74

DIARY

ALAN TITCHMARSH
Meets
HRH PRINCE PHILIP

Titchmarsh: As he approaches his ninetieth birthday, Prince Philip shows little sign of slowing down. The Queen's consort is, by anyone's standard, something of a phenomenon. His natural exuberance and energy would exhaust a man half his age. It is one of the great privileges not only of my life but my children's lives that he has agreed to meet me on what is – remarkably – the eve of his 90th birthday, when, it must be said, he shows little sign of slowing down!

Sir, would I be right in thinking that, as you approach your 90th birthday, you show little sign of slowing down!!

Prince Philip: What a fatuous thing to say! You need your head examined. Why should I? I mean, if you've got nothing better to ask...?!

Titchmarsh: Ho, ho, ho! Marvellous, sir! You certainly show little sign of slowing down! Now, might I take you back to your childhood, sir! By all accounts, it was, in Royal terms, pretty unconventional!

Prince Philip: Depends what you mean by unconventional. Damn fool question. Is there much more of this?

Titchmarsh: Am I right in thinking, sir, that, as a child, you were, by all accounts, something of a handful?

Prince Philip: Who ARE you? Who IS he? Are you the chauffeur? Get me away from here!

Titchmarsh: Excellent! Now, you were born nearly ninety years ago, sir. That's a remarkable achievement, especially for someone of your advanced years. Does it really feel that long?

Prince Philip: Ghastly little man. Haven't the foggiest who he is.

Titchmarsh: I am now hugely privileged to be in the gracious presence of Her Royal Highness Princess Anne the Princess Royal. Thank you kindly for having me, ma'am, and may I say at once –

Princess Anne: Is there much more of this?

Titchmarsh: Your father is, if I may say so, ma'am, obviously a truly remarkable man, ninety years young! May I ask you, ma'am, what it felt like growing up with such a truly remarkable man as your father?

Princess Anne: If you must.

Titchmarsh: What did it feel like, ma'am, growing up with such a truly remarkable man as your father?

Princess Anne: Perfectly stupid question. What do you THINK it felt like? I didn't have another father to compare him to, did I?

Titchmarsh: An excellent answer, ma'am! Some say, ma'am, that your father is not the type to suffer fools gladly?

Princess Anne: Insufferable question.

Titchmarsh: Might I now be so bold as to ask you, ma'am, whether having Prince Philip as a father meant that –

Princess Anne: Time up! I haven't got all day. Run along.

Titchmarsh: Thank you most graciously, ma'am! It's been a huge privi-

Princess Anne: Next!

Posh Old Lady: More tea? Back in those days, Philip was a young man, oh, very much so. He did the sort of things that were the sort of things we all did at the time. But of course, that was a good many years ago. As time went orn, he grew older, as we all did. Oh, very much so. In many ways, he's the same now as he was then. As we all are. Though in other ways, he is rather different. As we all are. Oh, very much so.

Titchmarsh: Tell me about your naval career, sir.

Prince Philip: It was a career. And it was naval. Nothing more to say.

Titchmarsh: There must have been some amusing or exciting moments?

Prince Philip: Quite possibly.

Titchmarsh: Do any spring to mind, sir?

Prince Philip: No.

Titchmarsh: Marvellous! Then, in 1947, you married Her Royal Highness the Queen.

Prince Philip: What's it to do with you?

Gyles Brandreth: The Duke's sense of humour is truly second to none. In all the years I've known him, he's always been HUGELY amused by my repartee. It's one of his most appealing characteristics, and one for which, frankly, he's far too seldom given credit. I once saw him ROARING with laughter when an underling stepped on a corgi and fell over backwards, breaking his neck!

Titchmarsh: You are now, sir, by my reckoning, the longest serving consort in British history. What does that mean to you?

Prince Philip: What does what mean? Get on with it, man!

Titchmarsh: The fact that you are now the longest serving consort in British history, sir. What does that mean to you?

Prince Philip: What on earth do you think it means? How long is a piece of string? What's the square root of 29? How am I meant to know? Are you completely daft? Who do you think I am? What's the point? Where's the sense? Who are you? What the hell are you doing here?

Who let him in?!

As told to CRAIG BROWN

Public service strike
MARCHERS CONDEMNED
By Our Industrial Staff **Sir Robin Day of Action**

CONSERVATIVE Cabinet Office Minister Francis Maude has condemned thousands of marchers who descended on central London for not resorting to violence and running street battles with police.

"No one wants to see reasonable and measured protests where the strikers air real grievances over their dwindling living standards. It was shameful that this march wasn't obscured by anarchists in gas masks and Womble outfits running street battles with riot police while posh rock stars' kids are daubing graffiti over Churchill's statue," he said.

I had to bring my kids because some selfish sods closed the school

I don't want to keep striking after I'm 66

Come on, pay attention, or I'll have to get cross

"You were right, my love, never throw anything away"

HEATH

DIANA AT 50

What would the world have been like if Tina Brown hadn't written her piece about what the world would have been like if Diana hadn't died and had lived to be 50.

By **Tina Brown**

How Diana might have looked

If Princess Diana had not tragically died in that tragic tunnel in tragic Paris she would undoubtedly still be alive. She would no doubt have been best friends with Uncle Gary Middleton, would have won 'Strictly Come Dancing' hosted by Sir Bruce Forsyth and would have remarried at least twice to Shane Warne and Prince Albert of Monaco.

She would obviously have been canonised by Pope Benedict for her work discovering a cure for cancer and would have been the first female astronaut to land on Mars.

And of course we would all be anticipating her coronation when an embarrassed Prince Charles would have stood aside to make her the Queen of Hearts.

That much we all know. But the most important aspect of Diana's life at 50 would have been the fact that she would definitely not have to read this sort of rubbish by myself.

© Tina Brownose, 2011, 2012, 2013 etc.

"Obviously, Olaf's death has come as a tremendous shock to all of us in the pillaging community"

The Memoirs of Lord Rees-Mogg

No one was closer to the British Establishment than the ultimate insider – William Rees-Mogg, who saw the defining events of the last sixty years at first hand. With his all-seeing eye and laser-sharp political perception, Mogg was the man at the centre of every storm. Read him all next week, only in The Times.

Monday

The Queen A gracious lady. I met her only once, but it was enough for me to judge her as the most gracious lady I had ever met. Apart from Mrs Gandhi, whom I never did meet but saw once on television. She was frequently mentioned in The Times, of which I was the editor.

Tuesday

Harold Wilson When I met him I could not help noticing that he spoke with a funny accent, which I took to be evidence of his northern background.

Wednesday

Richard Nixon A delightful man whom I found to be a statesman of great vision and personal integrity. I met him on one occasion and he kindly tape-recorded our conversation.

Thursday

Mick Jagger One of the founders of the Thatcherite revolution and, like myself, an admirer of John Stuart Mill. My daughter, Amoretta, once met him on holiday in the Galapagos Islands. She found him quite charming.

Friday

Gordon Brown One of the very few Prime Ministers whom I did not meet, but had I done so, I would no doubt have found nothing interesting to say about him.

Saturday

Mao Tse Tung Chairman Mao has been unjustly maligned in my opinion. It was my privilege to be granted an official audience in order that I might impress upon him the merits of Sky Television. Mao had a first-rate mind and immediately grasped exactly what I was proposing, asking what was in it for him?

Sunday

Rupert Murdoch I have always admired Mr Murdoch, ever since he became my employer. His decision to serialise this worthless, pooterish pile of self-serving drivel in his excellent newspaper, only goes to confirm my high opinion of myself *(Surely Mr Murdoch? Ed.)*

© William Rees-Smugg, The Waste of Times 2011.

ED MILIBAND

Where do you stand on the issue of spoons?

Look, I'm all for spoons and the right of people to have spoons but we have to accept that demanding too many spoons in the current climate serves no useful purpose.

So you're against spoons?

No, all I'm saying is that I'm all for spoons and the right of people to have spoons but we have to accept that demanding too many spoons in the current climate serves no useful purpose.

Have spoons played a large role in your life?

I don't think it's particularly helpful to look backward what I think *is* important is I'm all for spoons and the right of people to have spoons but we have to accept that demanding too many spoons in the current climate serves no useful purpose.

Do you have a favourite spoon?

I would like to make it clear that I don't believe in singling out one spoon in preference to others what I *do* believe is that I'm all for spoons and the right of people to have spoons but we have to accept that demanding too many spoons in the current climate serves no useful purpose.

Has anything amusing ever happened to you in connection with a spoon?

It's all very easy to laugh at spoon-related incidents but what is more difficult is to be clear that I'm all for spoons and the right of people to have spoons but we have to accept that demanding too many spoons in the current climate serves no useful purpose.

Thank you very much.

NEXT: *David Miliband "Me and My Spoon which my brother stole from me".*

"I'm going to take you off nights, Johnson"

RATKO MLADIC DEFENCE 'TOO FEEBLE'

LAWYERS for Ratko Mladic, the former Bosnian Serb general facing war crimes charges, have called for the proceedings to be stopped, his defence being far too feeble to survive the rigours of a trial.

"I have never seen such a sickly defence," said one lawyer. "My worry is that Mladic's defence will barely make it through the first retelling of the Srebrenica massacre before collapsing and dying right in front of us.

"No defence this weak should ever be allowed within a thousand miles of a courtroom." *Reuters*

I was only obeying my own orders

THE EYE'S MOST READ STORIES

Tories abandon weekly rubbish policy

The Conservatives have confirmed that in the wake of embarrassing U-turns on welfare, the NHS and prison reform, they are abandoning weekly rubbish policies.

"We know this could cause a massive stink within the party, but we believe it's what the public wants", said Communities Minister Eric Pickles. "They seem quite content to throw away a new rubbish Tory policy every two weeks, rather than reverting to the old once a week collection.

"We must cut down on the number of rubbish Tory policies being consigned to landfill after yet another embarrassing U-turn."

That Liz Jones Face Lift In Full

Before

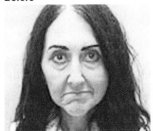

After

PLUS

● Should the Mail on Sunday have a face lift and lose all those awful lines written by Liz Jones? **94**

C of E Gives Go-Ahead to 'Bearded Bishops'

By our Religious Affairs Correspondent **Ruth I. Was Gled-Hill**

THE GENERAL Synod has today approved by a slim majority of 294-293 the ordination of bearded bishops – but only if they agree "never to shave".

In what was described as a major breakthrough, a spokesman called the ruling "a landmark decision allowing the church to go forward and concentrate on the real issues confronting the Church today, ie homosexuality."

Celibate-by-Date

A new motion before the Synod calls for the ordination of women as bishops "providing they are men" and for "black bishops" providing they are white. *(Is this right? Ed.)*

GNOME 24 — THE PAGE YOU CAN READ 24 HOURS A DAY

SUICIDE 'INCREASES RISK OF DEATH' claims anti-suicide organisation...... KATE MIDDLETON 'continues to wear clothes' claims onlooker... special report... ADMIRAL says under-funded Navy will be 'unable to protect Ascot Ladies Day'.... more soon... CANCER a terrible thing' says Prime Minister...... more soon..... RUGBY PLAYER has rowdy stag night... more soon.. LADY WEARS HAT More soon......

The Adventures of Mr Milibean

Fountain & Jamieson

77

Olympic Ticketing Fiasco 'A Success'

by Our Olympic Staff **Phil Corporate-Box**

The organisers of the 2012 Olympic ticketing fiasco say the fiasco went off without a hitch.

"Many long months of planning went into making the process for applying for tickets as labyrinthine and tortuous as possible," said a man who looks like he probably runs about a lot.

"It takes meticulous attention to detail to make sure that the millions of people who wanted to get a ticket were unable to log on to the 2012 site, let alone get one."

The organisers admitted there was a brief glitch during the second round of the lottery when hackers attacked the site and briefly made it work properly, allowing people to get tickets for events they wanted to see, but this was quickly blocked and normal chaos was resumed.

There was joy, however, for Nike, Adidas and Coke, as they discovered they'd got all the tickets they'd hoped for to the very best events at the 2012 Olympics.

Golden Moments

"Thousands of tickets to the Opening Ceremony, the swimming finals, the 100 metres men's sprint final and the cycling," said all the delighted multi-national corporations. "This is like a dream come true.

"We can't believe how simple and easy it has been to get all the tickets we wanted and more. We just hope everyone's experience was as simple and stress free as ours."

THE JOHANN HARI INTERVIEW

This Week: **The late Winston Churchill**

The familiar features of Britain's most famous war-time Prime Minister break into a smile as he offers me a cup of tea in his elegant Chartwell drawing room.

I ask him how he feels about the country's current debt crisis.

"Never in the field of human conflict has so much been owed by so many to so few', says Churchill puffing on his trademark cigar.

I change the subject and question the pugnacious elder statesman about the present conflict in Libya. He thinks for a minute and then answers slowly:

"We shall fight them on the beaches, we shall fight them on the landing grounds, we shall fight them in the fields and streets, we shall fight in the hills." He adds, "We shall never surrender".

Trenchant views as ever from the iconic historian-come-polititian. But what does he really think of Ed Miliband?

"A modest man", he quips, "who has much to be modest about." I laugh and decide to tackle the most important and most controversial issue confronting Britain today:

"Sir Winston", I ask, "if a journalist such as myself uses quotes that he copies out from a subject's previous writings and pretends the interviewee said them at the time – and then gets caught – do you think it is the end of his career?"

He looks at me for a long time and then says in his unmistakable bulldog Churchillian voice,

"Johann this is not the end, it is not even the beginning of the end but it is perhaps the end of the beginning".

© *Johann Hari-Kiri 1945*

Where The Wild Things Aren't

Stark Warning For Johann Hari About Journalists Who Fake Stories

BORIS THE BONK ENGINE

BY THE REV. W. TAWDRY

"**L**OOK at me!" shouted Dave the Highspeed Train. "I'm sleek and shiny and I can go far faster than all you smelly old trains." And he whizzed through the Green Belt knocking down people's houses and running over the protestors. "Nothing can stop me!" tooted Dave.

But Boris the Bonk Engine was furious. "We'll see about that!" he huffed and puffed. "Dave is just showing off because he thinks he's new and clever. But watch me!"

And, as the other trains looked on, Boris chuffed his way up behind Dave giving him a terrific shunt up the backside into the sidings.

"Help, I've come off the rails," cried Dave.

"Ha! Ha!" snorted Boris triumphantly. "You're not going so fast now that you've hit the buffers."

The End

© Rev. W. Nimby. 2011

"It's a breakthrough in care for the elderly"

Latin Phrases For Beginners

Pro Bono = For the good of yourself, tax-free, not in the service of the public, without wider obligation. e.g. *'He was wearing stupid sunglasses pro bono'* (Glastonbury 2011)

Next week: Cui Bono

BRITAIN'S GOT TALENT 'FIX'

Whatever happens, this man always wins

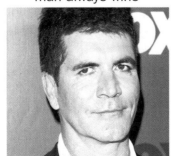

Notes & queries

Why have the Beckhams called their daughter Harper Seven?

● Mrs Ludmilla Rusbridger is quite wrong to claim that the child is named after the publisher HarperCollins who produced "The Posh Nosh Diet Book" (2006) and "More Posh Nosh" (2008). The Harper in question is, of course, the actor Gerald Harper, perhaps best known for his role as Adam Adamant (ITV 1966) which was a great favourite with David's nan, Becky Beckham. And as for his theory that the name Seven is a romantic reference to the restroom of the 7/11 store in Malibu where the baby was quite possibly conceived – arrant nonsense and offensive to boot! Seven is of course a tribute to David's erstwhile friend and mentor, the former England manager, Seven Goran Eriksson.

The Rev J.P. Lovehandle

● I'm afraid Rev. Lovehandle is once again making a fool of himself and showing his ignorance of popular culture. Harper Seven is of course the restricted military zone in New Mexico where aliens first landed in 1948. The Beckhams are members of the Harper Seven Society who believe that the US Government has consistently covered up the existence of extra-terrestrials whilst experimenting on them for the purposes of bio-weaponry development.

Professor Juliard d'Assange

● Oh dear, oh dear. The potty professor will have to accept a rather more prosaic answer to the vexed question of the Beckham baby's nomenclature. Victoria Beckham, as everyone knows, is an accomplished amateur harp player who has performed at private parties for their Royal Highnesses the Earl and Countess of Wessex on many occasions. And her favourite piece? Pepperoni's Harp Concerto Number 7 in D Minor (1758). Mystery solved, I'm afraid!

Maj. Gen. John Major-General

Answers to the following please:

Why were the Magnificent Seven so called? Exactly how many Samurai were there in the Japanese classic "The Seven Samurai"? Do fewer than seven people read the Spectator?

The Eye's Controversial New Columnist

The columnist with teeth. Three of them

This week I am extremely angry about the Beckhams and their naming of their baby "Harper 7". Speaking as a baby myself *(see photo)*, I am all too aware of the pain this can cause. Many of my nursery colleagues have been given ridiculous names that will surely bring derision on them in later life, names such as "Apple" and "Cruz". Why can't these parents think for a moment, and give them fine, honourable names like "Rupert" or "James"? Good honest names which will guarantee that they will grow up as fine, upstanding citizens, such as my name, which is *(cont. p. 94)*

"I don't like it when mummy and daddy fight"

GOTCHA!

MURDOCH GOES DOWN WITH ALL HACKS

Saturday 16 July

We are sorry.

We are sorry that we have been caught.

We are sorry that we had to close down the News of the World.

We are sorry that we can't take over BSkyB.

We deeply regret that our share price has gone down as a result of previous wrong-doing by some individuals in our employ.

I was personally shocked and appalled to find out the kind of thing that had been going on in my business.

I thought of my dear old mother and how appalled she must be that the family company is now going down the toilet.

I can hear the old lady say, "Jeez, Rupert, you've made a dingo's bollocks of the whole thing."

I apologise for the hurt that has been caused to those most closely affected by these issues... ie my family and myself.

Sincerely (no really),

[signature]

Rupert Murdoch

⊕ News International

Sunday 17 July

We are sorry again.

We are sorry that yesterday's apology didn't fool anyone.

But this apology is intended to put the record straight once and for all.

News International is in the business of making apologies. We are proud of the many apologies we have issued over the last five days. However, in this instance, our apology yesterday clearly fell short of the high standard of apologies that our company has traditionally maintained.

We apologise for this apology and have taken steps to ensure that in future all our apologies meet the criteria which our readers expect.

We are determined to put things right and there will be further apologies in the weeks to come, if this one doesn't wash either.

Sincerely (no, really this time),

[signature]

Rupert Murdoch

⊕ News International

This apology has been produced in collaboration with communication strategists Bullshite, Whitewash and Koverupp of New York.

K.J.Lamb

WORLD'S GREATEST NEWSPAPER CLOSES

'I was there' says Lunchtime O'Screws

Wapping, Saturday

Grown men wept. Women wailed. And toddlers asked, "Is it really the end, Daddy?"

What they thought could never happen had come tragically true. One of Britain's finest and most respected institutions had come crashing to the ground.

As the presses rolled for the last time, I was witnessing with my own eyes not just the end of an era but the end of a whole way of life.

The News of the World was as British as fish and chips, the Routemaster bus and chicken tikka masala.

The end of the News of the World is nigh

Millions of devoted readers will now have literally nothing to do on a Sunday without what George Orwell called "the most important contribution to English Literature since Shakespeare".

Yet I saw the brave men and women of the paper's staff, who have served their country so well, marching out of the building with their heads held high.

Said one, who was wearing the traditional robes of an Arab sheikh and carrying concealed in his headdress the legendary tools of his trade – a secret camera and tape recorder, "It has been an extraordinary privilege to be part of this magnificent newspaper and to be allowed to entrap drunken minor members of the Royal Family into providing us with front-page scoops."

Burnoose of the World

Every one of these fine journalists was saying the same thing. "We do not blame Mr Murdoch or his son James or their friend Rebekah for closing down the paper and putting us all out of work at no notice in order to save their skins.

"This is the nature of the business. And, besides, we are all hoping to be re-employed again next month, when Mr Murdoch launches the Sun on Sunday."

ON OTHER PAGES

● *Paediatricians can now come out of hiding and roam freely across the country again by Rebekah Brooks p. 94*

168 YEARS OF GREATNESS

IN 1829 the News of the World was founded by a Wapping ironmonger Samuel Filth (later Lord Filth of Wapping). His formula was simple – to provide the newly-literate British working classes with "a bit of smut to read on a Sunday afternoon after going to church".

Filth's world-beating formula was a potent mix of sex, murder, more sex and more murders.

Over the decades, the new paper's headlines painted an incomparable picture of the mores of a changing Britain.

"My night of shame with churchwarden's wife – runaway vicar tells all" 1862

"Vicar's wife found dead in bath – is he the Ripper?" 1889

"Vicar murdered by wife after his unnatural acts with choirboy" 1911

"Vicar in cocaine-fuelled 3-in-a-bed love romps with footballer and TV weather girl" 2011

Here, in just a few vivid, beautifully-crafted words we can see reflected our entire island story over the past two centuries.

And now, with the tragic and untimely demise of the best-selling newspaper in the English-speaking world, who is left to record for posterity the most significant national events of this and any other time?

No one – and the rest is silence.

NEVER TOO OLD

A new love story by Dame Sylvie Krin

THE STORY SO FAR: Ageing media mogul Rupert Murdoch has flown into Britain to take personal charge of the crisis enveloping his empire. Now read on...

"JEEZ! Surely that's enough," wheezed the elderly antipodean tycoon as he hobbled around the Serpentine in his designer Grandadidas tracksuit and baseball hat bearing the legend "I ❤ Attack", a present from his beautiful young oriental wife from the land of the pot noodle.

"How bloody far have we run now?" he croaked, as his young, blonde personal trainer tried to drag him along the path.

"About twenty yards," she encouraged. "You're doing really well. Only another ten miles to go."

At that moment, Rupert's Bad Apple i-phone rang with its distinctive "Funeral March" ringtone which his children had given to him for his 80th birthday. With a sense of overpowering relief, he broke off his training session to speak to his beloved Wendi.

"Lupert!" came the familiar bark. "What you doing now, old man?"

"I'm doing what you said, darling," soothed the octogenarian billionaire. "I'm showing everyone that I'm a fit person."

"No, you bruddy fool – you should be running company, not running round park..."

"But you're always encouraging me to pursue vigorous exercise, my sweet and sour saucepot," he soothed.

"Shurrup, Lupert, and risten. You sort out mess first – before we lose all our money. Way things going, Dim Sun James and froozy Lebekah screw up entire company, so Wendi inherit *no* fortune cookie."

Rupert sighed, the weight of the years suddenly heavy on his shoulders, as heavy as the backpack full of bricks which the trainer had insisted he carry...

"Whatever you say, my little dragon lady, I'll get right onto it."

The voice from America softened slightly. "Good. You save company *then* you do New York Marathon, ok?"

(To be continued...)

COMMENT

Time to move on

THE phone hacking saga has run its course. As revelation has followed revelation the nation has become increasingly weary of this story. It may fascinate the Westminster village but Middle England has more serious matters with which to concern themselves such as the frequency of wheelie bin rubbish collection and the calamitous fall in house prices due to the current financial crisis.

Surely it is now time to draw a line under this unsavoury matter before further details emerge about the Daily Mail and the Mail on Sunday being up to exactly the same kind of dirty tricks in the dark arts of journalism department?

On Other Pages

● Why don't we focus on the real criminals of this story – the BBC **by Melanie Phillips** p2

● Why we mustn't be too hard on press barons like Rupert Murdoch and, er, Lord Rothermere **by Steven Glovepuppet** p3

● It's all a storm in a teacup **by Peter McPhone-Hackey** p94

This Week's Latest Inquiries In Full

1 Judge-led inquiry into role of News International journalists in "Hackergate" scandal

2 Judge-led inquiry into the role of the police in "Knackergate" scandal

3 Judge-led inquiry into wider press ethics, finding that all journalists should be locked up or strung up because it is the only language they understand

4 Parliamentary inquiry into the relations between politicians and News International, finding that all MPs had behaved honourably at all times

5 Parliamentary inquiry into why Keith Vaz MP was not entirely the most appropriate person to chair an inquiry into corruption, shiftiness and general malfeasance, finding that if you say this, he will accuse you of being a racist

6 Judge and Parliamentary-led inquiry into all the other inquiries, finding that there is a pressing need for further inquiries into *(cont. 2094)*

TV HIGHLIGHTS

All channels 10pm

Midsummer Murdoch

In the sleepy village of Chipping Norton the bodies are beginning to pile up. First it was mild-mannered ex-journalist Andy Coulson, then the flame-haired beauty Rebekah, wife of local race-horse trainer "Champagne Charlie" Brooks.

Inspector Barnaby is called in to investigate and attends a dinner party hosted by local celebrity and racing car driver Jeremy Clarkson. Other guests include the shifty local politician, Prime Minister David Cameron and his glamorous wife Samantha as well as seedy PR man Matthew Freud and his blonde bombshell wife, Liz Murdoch – not to mention her brother James who seems to have plenty to hide. Are they all in it up to their necks? Are they all guilty of Murdoch Most Foul?

Just as the Inspector gets close to identifying the guilty

Rebekah and Charlie at the village fete

men and women, he himself is arrested for his close links with everyone mentioned above.

● Who will be next? Viewers will have to wait for next week to find out "Whodunnit"! (Everyone)

CAST IN FULL

Rebekah Brooks .... Catherine Tate
Charlie Brooks .... Nigel Havers
Andy Coulson ....Ben Wishaw
James Murdoch ....Daniel Radcliffe
Jeremy Clarkson ....Jim Broadbent
Liz Murdoch .... Hermione Norris
Rupert Murdoch ..... Barry Humphries
Inspector Barnaby....Lord Stephenson

News Corpse

ROBERT THOMPSON

KNACKER LASHES NEWS INTERNATIONAL

APPEARING before a committee of MPs, Inspector "Knacker of the Yard" Knacker today launched a ferocious attack on senior News International executives for failing to cooperate with his inquiry into the original inquiry into phone hacking.

The inspector told MPs how he personally spent over 10 minutes trying to phone Mr James Murdoch to ask him whether any of his employees had engaged in phone hacking, only to be told by his secretary that Mr Murdoch was at a meeting.

"Mr Murdoch never rang me back," said the inspector. "Here we have a global media conglomerate seeking to obstruct the course of justice at the very highest level by withholding cooperation with the police."

Asked by the committee if he had attempted to contact Mr Murdoch again before writing his report exonerating News International, the inspector explained, "You do not realise that, at that very time, I was engaged in dealing with several major terrorist threats, any one of which could have brought civilisation as we know it to an end.

"I did not therefore have time to deal with what seemed a very trivial and unimportant issue, ie a few celebrities getting upset about their phone messages being intercepted."

When the Committee asked why he was not too busy to have a number of dinners with senior News International executives, the inspector replied, "It would have looked suspicious if I had turned down a perfectly bona fide invitation to enjoy dinner at the Ritz from a company into whose activities I was conducting an investigation. The public would rightly have thought I was failing in my duty if I had not turned up and consumed the fine wines for which that particular establishment is well known."

Asked if he had ever accepted money from News International, Inspector Knacker threw up his hands in horror and said, "This is an absolutely outrageous allegation. To suggest that a senior police officer would personally take money from a news organisation is a total insult – as I made clear in my column for the News of the World on several occasions."

The Inquiry continues.

LATE NEWS
KNACKER RESIGNS

IN A sensational development Inspector Knacker has now offered his resignation and issued the following statement.

"Evening, all. My personal integrity is intact. I am not losing any sleep over my honesty and integrity which as I say is intact.

I feel very good about myself due to a long stay in the excellent health spa Champagneys, whose world-renowned relaxation techniques include drinking large amounts of free champagne.

May I make it clear that at no time was I aware of any link between the former News of the World journalist Mr Wally Wolfman and my PR consultant Mr Wolfy Wallman.

I am entirely confident that I had no idea that hiring Mr Wolf was in any way a conflict of interest with my investigations which would compromise my integrity which as I say is entirely in tatters, correction intact. That is why I am resigning forthwith. Mind how you go."

LATE, LATE NEWS
ANOTHER KNACKER RESIGNS

(That's enough, Ed)

IT'S A FAIR COP!

Goodbye, Goodbye, Goodbye

"We're all in it together!"

Mayor of London
Boris Johnson
writes on the crisis facing the Metropolitan Police

Cripes! There's only one chap emerged with any credit from this palaver and that's yours truly – Bojo! I called in the top rozzers at the Met as soon as I got wind of something fishy going on and I tore them off a strip.

I said, "You chumps! Why did you hire this Wallis chappie as your PR wallah when you knew he was from the News of the World, who *you* were meant to be putting the cuffs on?!"

All credit to them. They fell on their swords like noble Romans, admitting that they should take responsibility for being hugger-mugger with a bad 'un!

But, I hear you ask, shouldn't the same rules apply to our friend in Downing Street who hired chummy Coulson as his PR man when he knew he had been up to no good at the News of the World?

You know, I don't like bad-mouthing an old school chum (and fellow Buller!), but, crikey, shouldn't Dave follow the coppers' excellent example and do the decent thing?! Thus letting a more suitable, better chap take over. Someone who's got a bit more noodle-power in the grey matter department and who would make a better fist of it than Calamity Dave!

And, incidentally, someone without any skeletons in the cupboard – because they have all come out already!!

No prizes for guessing who that might be, eh, what?

Bozza
(Friend of the Rozzers)

DIARY

KEITH RICHARDS

I don't wannna knock the guy cos I love him like a brother but Mick's full of shit I mean like I'm just hangin loose and shootin up and blowin crap and he's just like wooh look at me guys wooh I'm Jumpin Jack Flash pout pout yeah look at me I'm Mick fuckin Jagger I'm Mick I'm dancin round the stage like a ponce and I'm like no you're not you're just a turd with a banana stuffed up his pants I'm the one they all love I'm the fuckin genius legend I'm the one they come to see I'm the Stones man and you're just the little wanker who flits about doin twirls like you're one of Pan's fuckin People or whatever like gimme a break man it's me who's the spirit of the Sixties it's me they wanna know about it's me who's so fuckin laidback and hangin loose and doin all kind of nuts things but I love Mick like a brother him and me we been together since the early Sixties yeah that was a decade to remember right we had some good shit in the Sixties like me and Anita Pallenwodever we went boinky boinky boinky for like weeks on end boinky boinky boinky mornin noon and night well not mornin cos we was zonked out and not noon cos we like hadn't woken up and not night cos we was clean out of it totally gone but all the rest of the time we was boinky boinky boinky boinky boinky boink that was before Mick like comes along when I'm not lookin' and starts his shit with her I mean I love the guy like a brother but he never meant nothin to Anita nothin nothin nothin she just saw him as my backin singer the freak who gets in the way while I'm like playin guitar...

...but then that's the Sixties its the decade that came right after the Seventies no yeah no nice one son lemme see the Seventies was the one that came before the Nineties and the Sixties came between the Eighties and the Nineties and the Fifties was the one which was after the Sixties but before the Seventies so by my recknin it goes like Sixties Fifties Nineties Eighties Seventies nah that can't be right because the Seventies definitely came before the Eighties otherwise it would be called the Nineties jeez who the fuck cares its just numbers the whole thing's just like an Establishment conspiracy man they're shit scared of the Stones they don't want the whole applecart whatevered so they try and muddle us with numbers and decades and years and blah blah blah and all that kinda numbers crap so's to make us like automatons or whatever so the revolution they was dreadin might never happen because they've like zonked us out with their fuckin sums so we can't remember nothin but then what people don't understand right is my memory's just amazin just amazin go on ask me somethin ask me anythin like ask me about everythin that happened in the Sixties and I'll tell you right okay you wanna know what happened in the Sixties right easy man the Sixties was the decade we really got out of our heads and the other thing that happened in the Sixties aw come on now there must of been something else happened in the Sixties yeah that's it we really got out of our heads...

...and there's another thing about the Sixties while we're on the whatever jeez you think you can remember nothin and then one memory triggers another and before you know it there's 600 rounds of memories per second spoolin out but I'll never forget The Beatles the so-called fuckin Beatles shit band there was John George Ringo and whatsit and they all had small todgers and couldn't sing and couldn't play and none of them ever got off with Anita not once well except maybe for Ringo oh yeah and p'raps John too and George but she told me she didn't even enjoy doin it with them at least not much and anyway no-one remembers The Beatles now no-one could give a fuckin shit about them they're even more of a total bummer than Mick though I love the guy like a brother but he's totally up his own arse...

...I don't want to knock Mick but all the songs we so-called wrote together weren't written by him they were written by me like dada dadada dadada da da da dada the openin bars of Satisfaction they just came to me like out of the clear blue fuckin sky like 9/11 and all that shit dada dadada dadada da da da dada shit it like all just came together and I'm thinkin whoa I'm thinkin whoa this riff's gonna change history it's like the Battle of Britain and the six chicks of Henry 8th and the Magna Blah Blah Blah all rolled into one and don't get me wrong I love Mick like a brother but that fuckin asshole shouldn't take the credit cos it was all me there should be a law against it and Mick's just a fuckin piece of small dick crap but hey I'm cool about it I'm really cool and anyway Anita gave me a blow job first I got it first I did I did he was way behind and my book's earned four fuckin million and his hasn't even been written yet so he's lookin pretty fuckin small now but hey who cares man I'm just laid back I'm just like so fuckin totally laid back hey man I'm cool.

As told to CRAIG BROWN

AID AGENCIES WARN OF BLAH... BLAH... BLAH...

by Our International Staff **Kate Emergency-Adie**

THERE was a growing sense of doom in the Horn of Africa as aid agencies warned of 'blah... blah... blah...'.

"No, we didn't say 'blah... blah... blah'", one aid agency worker insisted, "we said...", but unfortunately no one was listening to the rest of his sentence, as it was about something happening a long, long way away.

Aid agencies said they would continue to highlight the humanitarian disaster unfolding to a jaded British public, who responded quickly by saying that all they could hear was them saying 'blah... blah... blah...'.

Notes & queries

What is the origin of the Snow Leopard cocktail served at the recent wedding of Zara Phillips and England rugby player Mike Tindall?

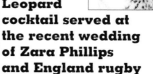

The Snow Leopard consists of two parts of the African Liqueur Bwanakil (made from the fermented juice of the Baobab fruits), two parts scotch whisky and a thimble full of anti-freeze all topped with grated coconut shell. It was devised by the late Ernest Hemingway and is mentioned in his famous short story *Kilimanjaro Safari 1936.* "Papa" Hemingway whom I had the privilege of meeting once in Nairobi was known to be able to drink 17 Snow Leopards without any visible signs of intoxication.

Samuel J. Horstwessel Junior, Michigan

Mr Horstwessel is sadly mistaken with his fanciful story about Hemingway. The Snow Leopard is a much more recent invention which only became popular with young royals in the last couple of years.

It is rumoured to contain the semi-legal drug Mau-Mau (PolyMethaKetaLone) in addition to Ribena, Marmite and of course Elderflower Cordial.

Credit for the cocktail must be given to veteran Channel 4 newsreader Jon Snow who is known in the newsroom as The Snow Leopard due to his white hair and colourful ties.

R.V.F. Guru-Murthy (no relation)

Answers to the following Olympic Special Notes & Queries next week:

When was croquet last an Olympic sport? Has the Vatican ever fielded an Olympic team? What is Johann Hari's real name?

A Life Tragically Cut Short

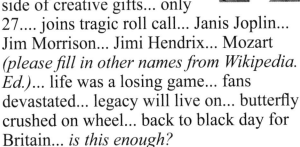

A life tragically cut short... troubled genius... precocious talent... inner demons... multiple addictions... rehab... self-destructive urges... dark side of creative gifts... only 27.... joins tragic roll call... Janis Joplin... Jim Morrison... Jimi Hendrix... Mozart *(please fill in other names from Wikipedia. Ed.)*... life was a losing game... fans devastated... legacy will live on... butterfly crushed on wheel... back to black day for Britain... *is this enough?*

THE 94 CLUB

THE TRAGIC death of the actress Googie Withers at the shockingly late age of 94 has created yet another new member of what has come to be known as "The 94 Club".

Miss Withers was merely one of that galaxy of outstanding cultural figures whose lives were suddenly cut tragically long at the fateful age of 94.

The star of 1940s revues joins an elite band of those other untroubled geniuses who never lived to see their 95th year.

The glittering roll call of fame includes the playwright Bernard Shaw, the novelist Anthony Powell, the legendary journalist Bill Deedes, the food connoisseur and bon viveur Egon Ronay, the inventor of Superglue, Harry Welsey Coover, and quite a lot of others whose names can be found on Wikipedia.

The question, as ever, remains the same. Why are so many of our great creative figures snatched from us at this particular age?

What is it about the number 94 that spells the end for so many *(cont. age 94)*

"Captain America isn't so impressive in the modern world economy"

CAN ADDICTION BE TREATED?

THE DEATH of Amy Winehouse has brought into stark focus the issue of addiction and how all Britain's tabloids were addicted to her.

"Occasionally the tabloids would be Amy free for a week or two and then there would be all this talk they'd kicked the habit for good", said one sub-editor, hastily stitching together a 12-page tribute to the singer. "But then they go on another three-day binge again, publishing every photo and story they could lay their hands on.

"Some hoped that Amy's death might be a turning point, but if anything it has only made the tabloid's addiction to Winehouse even worse."

Late News
Pete Doherty 'Still Alive'.

NORWAY

INSIDE THE MIND OF A KILLER

by criminologist **Dr Phil Space**

THE only way to truly understand the depraved actions of Anders Breivik is for us to go inside the mind of a killer.

And what do we find inside Anders' mind? How should I know? *(We're paying you for this rubbish – Ed)*...err... I mean, what we find inside the mind of a killer is that Anders was a pathetic loner *(I don't think he was – Ed)*...err, we find he was popular and gregarious *(Are you making this rubbish up as you go along? – Ed)*...okay, the main characteristic most killers share is their predisposition towards killing people *(You're Fired – Ed)*

Why I am not ashamed to have been quoted by Breivik

By Cab Driver and *Eye* columnist **Sid Snozzer** (Cab No. 1742382) .

Blimey guv! You can't blame me for that Norwegian nutter shooting all those people. I mean just 'cos he's lifted my ideas about immigration from one of my *Eye* columns doesn't mean that I am responsible does it? No, what I said was perfectly reasonable in context and I quote:

"All these Muslims flooding over here, taking our jobs, they should be strung up! It's the only language they understand 'cos they don't speak English do they, guv."

Now the loonies on the internet are having a go at me but I have made it clear that I condemn Breivik as a callous mass murderer. However, and this is the important thing, guv, a lot of what he says in his manifesto makes a lot of sense particularly the bit about Europe being overrun by Muslims who should be strung up. And besides I am not the only writer quoted with approval by Breivik – such distinguished names as John Stuart Mill, Simon Heffer and Adolf Hitler also appear in his manifesto.

I 'ad that Melanie Phillips in the back of the cab once, very nice lady. Not at all mad.

© *A Taxi Driver*

NEVER TOO OLD

A new love story by Dame Sylvie Krin, author of
Heir of Sorrows and Duchess of Hearts

THE STORY SO FAR: Octogenarian Ozzie oligarch Rupert Murdoch is desperately fighting to save his empire and has been summoned by a British Parliamentary Select Committee. Now read on...

"WAKE up, Lupert!" The shrill voice of his beloved Wendi stirred the elderly press potentate from his power snooze.

"You no sleep, old man. You answer question."

The suave, bespectacled inquisitor-in-chief, Tom Watswat MP, shuffled his papers expertly and fixed Rupert with his steely gaze.

"Would you like me to repeat the question, Mr Murdoch?"

The ageing antipodean rubbed his new designer Calvin McKenzie glasses on his striped Rebekah Brooks Brothers tie. What was it he was meant to say? What had the New York PR experts from Bullshite, Whitewash and Koverupp told him? Don't bumble? Or was it 'humble'? His once agile mind wandered... but then he felt a sharp stiletto in the ribs from behind and the soft voice of his Peking prawn cracker broke the silence.

"Remember, Lupert – you don't remember anything."

He gathered himself once again and his craggy features broke into a smile of relief as he answered the Torquemada of the Tearoom.

"I'm afraid I don't remember anything, sport, not even your bloody question."

A ripple of amusement ran around the oak-panelled Selwyn Lloyd Webber Committee Room.

The media moghul's confidence returned. He was damned if he was just going to sit back and take it like a swagman cornered with an empty billabong in the dunny.

"Here's something I *do* remember," he

added, banging the table with the flat of his hand, "and that's how bloody useless you poms were at Gallipoli, drinking tea and eating cucumber sandwiches whilst Mel Gibson was single-handedly saving your whingeing arses."

But his fearless tirade was cut off by the no-nonsense chairman John Whitteringon: "Thank you very much indeed for coming,

Mr Murdoch. We know that you are a very busy man."

At that exact moment, a figure darted from the spectators' gallery, armed with a deadly custard pie and headed straight for the most powerful man in the world, hell bent on giving him a foam-based humiliation in front of billions of worldwide viewers of the BBC's Parliamentary Channel.

There was a flash of pink and, as if in slow motion, the incredible Wendi soared through the air like an avenging angel, like a bird of prey, and delivered a deadly karate chop to the assailant's head. Not for nothing had she trained for years under legendary martial arts master Bruce Ang Lee.

"You leave Lupert alone, fat boy" she cried.

And then, with a graceful somersault and reverse flip, she kicked the pie dish out of his hand and back into his ugly, hate-filled face.

"Now big joke on you, funny guy!"

As the would-be attacker crumpled to the floor, moaning in pain, the committee rose to their feet and applauded in unison.

"Bravo!", "Hoorah for the dragon lady", "Is it time for lunch?" – their cheers echoed through the dusty chambers of Westminster.

"Strewth, Wendi, my little China chopstick!" cried Rupert. "My heart is bursting with pride!"

"No heart burst yet, old man! I protect my investment! You save company first, then heart burst, okay?"

Rupert was overwhelmed with emotion and a sense of awe at his hot-and-sour-souperwoman.

"Jeez, Wendi, you've got more prawn balls than all the blokes in this room put together."

And feeling like a man ten years younger, he asked for a glass of water and his tablets...

(To be continued)

Surprise Winner of Apprentice
by our Media Staff **Alan Sugar-Daddy**

IN A shock result, the hopeless geek triumphed in the competition to go into business with the ageing multi-millionaire tycoon.

The self-confessed "be-spectacled nerd", James Murdoch, had failed all the tasks set him by his father, including the one where he was project manager and had to run News International. Viewers had been hugely entertained by his garbled nonsensical management-speak, his lack of people skills and his apparent

ignorance of everything that was going on at all times.

However when he went into the legendary boardroom, tough-talking Rupert Murdoch looked at his CV, asked him the killer question, "Are you my son?" and then shocked the world by saying, "you're hired."

And it was the glamorous female favourite, Rebekah, who had the famous finger pointed at her and was told, "You're fired!"

Said a delighted James, "Vectoring in the quantum feasibility leverage quotient I *(cont. p. 94)*

PIERS IN SHOCK HACKING CLAIM

He opened his mouth and now he's got the sack. Why didn't he keep quiet?

Whistleblower's Mother

LIB DEMS SLAM 'CAMERON'S LACK OF JUDGEMENT'

By Our Political Staff **Simon Hogwarts**

SENIOR Liberal Democrats who did not wish to be named due to the fact that no one knows who they are, yesterday severely criticised the Prime Minister's willingness to enter into close relationships with unsuitable and discredited individuals.

Said one, "Cameron will get into bed with anyone if he thinks it will advance his political career. No matter how unsavoury or compromised they are, he just doesn't care."

He continued, "I mean this is a man who formed a coalition with *us*. Talk about a catastrophic error of judgement."

Said another Lib Dem, "Cameron was warned repeatedly that we were untrustworthy and that taking on people like Nick Clegg would lead to disaster. But did he listen? No."

However a former spokesperson for the Prime Minister was quick to defend his ex-employer. Speaking to the Pentonville inhouse journal "News Of The Screws",

MrCoulson said, "It's easy, with hindsight, to attack David for his links with the Lib Dems but at the time he accepted their assurances that they were not a bunch of shifty chancers desperate for power. The fact that they later turned out to have fiddled their expenses, tried to pervert the course of justice over speeding fines and made him do u-turns on all his promises is irrelevant."

Prisoner 14795 continued, "David wanted to give the Lib Dems a second chance which reflects well on his qualities of compassion. I for one am standing by him even if he is keeping his distance from me."

The Prime Minister immediately issued a statement saying that he had never heard of Nick Clegg and had never met him except possibly at Rupert Murdoch's parties and even then he and Clegg had never discussed politics but stuck to non-controversial subjects such as pushing through the BSkyB deal.

KNAVE OF HEARTS REMOVED FROM TRADE POST

By Our Royalty Staff **Nicolas Witch**

THE Knave of Hearts who for the last ten years has travelled round nursery world as a roving ambassador promoting tarts, has been sensationally relieved of his duties.

The controversial knave known as Prince Andy-Pandy (or sometimes Prince Anky-Panky) was involved in an incident where a number of tarts went missing.

Despite the knave's private expression of regret that he had embarrassed the Queen of Hearts and a promise that he would "steal no more", the knave was sacked.

DAILY TELEGRAPH | Friday, 5 August 2011

Letters to the Editor

SIR – Like many of your readers, I was appalled by the sad events at Trent Bridge in the recent England vs India Test match when batsman Ian Bell was allowed to resume his innings despite clearly being run out. The rules *are* the rules and the game of cricket is nothing if the rules are not adhered to by teams and umpires alike.

Older readers will remember, as I do, the famous incident in the 1898 Test match between the All England Gentlemen's XI and the Maharajah of Pisspohr's Invitation XI at Abbotabad.

The English captain, Sir Pelham Whittam-Smith, had hit the ball towards the square leg boundary where it disappeared into a mongoose nest and the fielders were unable to retrieve it. The batsman, Sir Pelham, and his partner, Rev. C.J. Monbiot, continued to run between the wickets, as they were entitled to do, amassing a score of 373 before the ball was eventually dug out by local dhobi-wallahs using elephants. The English batsmen were heavily criticised at the time for unsportsmanlike behaviour, but back in England they were rightly fêted as heroes for correctly sticking to the regulations laid down by the MCC.

The current talk of Indian Captain Mr M.S. Dhoni having acted "magnanimously" and "in the spirit of the game" is wide of the mark.

Both Mr Dhoni and the Umpire were clearly taken to one side and warned, as a sporting gesture, that a number of English fans "knew where they lived".

Surely no more needs to be said.

Major General Isidore Gusset
The Old Pavilion,
Not Cricket St Thomas, Dorset.

The Adventures of Mr Milibean

Fountain & Jamieson

MILIBEAN'S NOT BEING RUBBISH THIS WEEK! HURRAY!

YOU, MR PRIME MINISTER, ARE A DISGRACE!

HENRY DAVIES

YOU SPENT YEARS COSYING UP TO AN UNELECTED BULLY JUST SO YOU COULD GET POWER!

YOU WOULD NEVER CATCH ME DOING SOMETHING LIKE THAT!

Tunis Times

TOTTENHAM SPRING SWEEPS BRITAIN
Cameron Regime Totters

by Our London Staff **Al Jaz-effem**

FOR the third night running, the streets of London and many other cities were filled with angry crowds of protestors in the greatest challenge to Britain's Conservative ruling order for decades.

The protestors, mainly young and co-ordinated by social media such as Twitter, seemed fearless in confronting Britain's hated police force, as they burned buildings, ransacked shops and attacked news reporters.

London's Burning

What was most impressive about the demonstrators was the articulacy with which they listed their demands.

One told me, "We want free trainers, free mobiles, free plasma TVs and any loose cash in the till."

Free At Last

As I watched a crowd of happy, smiling 13-year-olds experiencing the new-found freedom of liberating the goods from the shelves of Currys, it was only too obvious that many of London's policemen were more than sympathetic to the aspirations of the demonstrators.

I saw dozens of officers standing back, doing nothing but simply watching the protestors walk off down the street carrying huge piles of expensive electronic equipment as they shouted their

exuberant slogan "It's all free".

Make no mistake, the British uprising is one of the most significant political developments in the history of the western world.

It can only be days now before these brave young revolutionaries force Cameron and his corrupt clique of cronies to flee the country and seek asylum in a friendly Arab country such as Libya.

"England... warm beer and old maids bicycling to holy communion"

What They Said

Prominent Figures Give Their Verdict On The Riots That Have Shocked Britain

KEN LIVINGSTONE: There is no doubt in my mind as to where the blame lies for this – it's all the fault of Boris Johnson. As long ago as 2008 I predicted that if Boris became Mayor, London would soon be in flames and I was absolutely right. There is only one way to deal with this complex socio-economic and political problem. Bring back myself. Vote Red Ken in 2012. You know it makes sense.

PATRICK MERCER MP: As an ex-Army officer who served in Northern Ireland, I know a bit about how to deal with civil unrest. There is only one way to contain this sort of thuggery. Call in the Army and give them everything they need: rubber bullets, proper bullets, water cannon, real cannon, guided missiles, killer drones – no option should be ruled out, up to and including nuclear weapons.

DESMOND MORRIS, Zoologist: The reason

for what has happened is very simple. If millions of humans are herded together in cities and tower blocks, they go mad. What we need is for everyone to go back to living in the jungle in straw huts, in harmony with nature. Then we would see no more of this kind of thing on our television screens because we would no longer have televisions.

REV. J.C. FLANNEL: On the one hand, you know, it's very easy, isn't it, to condemn these young people for their apparently selfish and

anti-social actions? But on the other hand, we must recognise the very real sense of anger and alienation that they feel as they *(cont. p. 94)*

JOHN PRESCOTT: There can be no excuse for this behaviour and no justificating of what happened but the blame for the riotising and lootifying has to be put squarely at the feet of the Tory government who don't give a damn about the working classes because they all went to private public schools and swan around in great big houses playing croquet and having affairs with their secretaries dressing up in ermine robes and giving themselves titles forgetting about the really disadvantaged people of Britain such as myself.

TV'S CHARLES MOORE:
We all have particular

memories of the recent distressing scenes of disorder which have engulfed the capital this August. In my own case, I was purchasing a new silk hat at Heffer's in St James's, when a group of unruly youths broke into the shop and set fire to it, trampling my newly acquired hat in the process. They then revealed that they were members of a gang calling itself the Bullingdon Club and had travelled all the way from Oxford to "trash Heffers and give the jolly old customers a bit of wazz".

JOHANN HARI: As W.B. Yeats told me when I interviewed him last week, "Things fall apart, the centre cannot hold. Mere anarchy is loosed upon the world."

Daily Mail

Friday, August 19, 2011

BRITAIN AT MERCY OF GREED-CRAZED MOBS

By Our Political Staff
Phil Space

BRITAIN has been reduced to chaos by amoral gangs, looting and stealing everything they can lay their hands on.

These ruthless criminals are guided by no ethical principle and are motivated only by greed.

They feel they owe no loyalty or allegiance to the wider community and are happy to trash the country they grew up in. With no limit to their rapacity, they are wholly indifferent to the needs and concerns of ordinary people.

Who are these people whose avarice and selfishness are bringing Britain to the edge of an unimaginable abyss?

A leading social analyst told us, "They are what we sociologists

Anonymous gang members of parliament displaying their ill-gotten gains

calls Britain's new 'overclass' which is comprised of various social groups sharing a common lack of conscience.

"These include feral bankers grabbing vast bonuses, corrupt politicians fiddling their expenses, useless and overpaid public sector officials and incompetent policemen working for the News of the World."

How dare they compare these dreadful rioters to decent British rats?

by The World's Worst Columnist
Max Hastings

The rat gets bad press these days.

But I say he's a perfectly decent little fellow, with his twinkly eyes and long, bushy tail, going about his lawful business, breaking into bin bags when the council have failed to pick up your wheelie for the third week running.

Whatever you say about the

rat, I have far more respect for him and his friend than those mindless vermin who have recently been running amok in the streets of our once proud capital city.

These moronic thugs and cretins have never done a day's work in their lives and have only one aim in their miserable lives – to get something for nothing.

Please send my usual £5,000 cheque asap.

© Dacreballs 2011.

On Other Pages ● Riots blamed on plastic bag menace: Chief Constable praises *Mail* campaign **2** ● House prices plummet as riots continue **3** ● Nancy Dell'Olio flees riot-torn Britain for beach: bikini pics **4-30**

HISTORIC COVER URGES FULL COOPERATION WITH POLICE

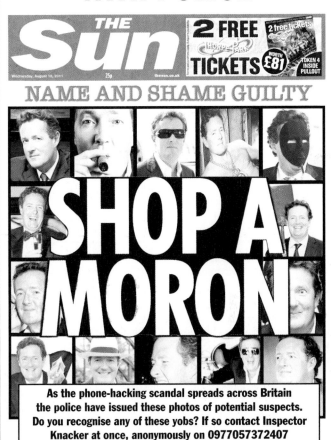

That BBC Riot Interview In Full

Presenter: Would you say it's all the fault of the cuts?

Expert: Well, no, there are a number of wider factors to be considered, including cultural and social issues which...

Presenter: So it's the cuts then?

Expert: No, I think we have to look beyond the...

Presenter: In short, very much the cuts to blame?

Expert: No, I...

Presenter: Thank you very much. Coming up next, more on the devastating effects of the cuts...

ANTI-SOCIAL NETWORKING

Riot Special

From The Message Boards

Members of the online community respond to the major issues of the day...

This poem came straight from the heart. I sent it to the paper but it was too real for them to publish.
London, Birmingham, Manchester too /
The riots have been so hard for you /
But there has been another side too /
All the good things that communities do / Heroes and helpers and here is the truth/ Great role models they for our so-troubled youth / Here is a thought for the long days to come/ Unite together and we'll sort out the scum.
I hope this brings some comfort to communities that are suffering.
– **Free_Spirit**

They have literally torn the heart out of the retail community. As one who has delivered PR for world class marquee malls as far afield as Birmingham and Manchester it appails me to see iconic brands assaulted in this way. Thank God Westfield was spared. – **Hattie**

lot's of trainer's for sale in Loot! lol!
– **Danny_Daz**

yes i was there an suddly o no its hapnin agen o no it's a riet yes i found some thing's an ete them but i don nofin bad – **hAnsolo**

Police should visit every single residence, and anyone with a new tv or trainers who cannot produce a receipt should be charged with handling stolen goods. If cells are overcrowded they can stand upright 24 hours a day if necessary. And yes, I DO have receipts for every single item in my house. – **Last_taxpayer_standing_in_the_LiebCon_socialist_paradise**

So water cannon are unsuitable for rioters who run and hide. Well excuse me but who the hell cares whether it suits the rioters? Use the bloody cannon and GET ON WITH IT! And if the cannon arrives too late, then go to their slums and blast them with it there. – **I_pay_but_have_no_say**

I'd like to see those rioters in the ring with Alan Minter. Best little boxer this country ever had and he spoke his mind about things you can't mention these days. – **The_Old_One-Two**

Three cheers for the great Clapham clean-up! We live in Clapham and dh and I had no hesitation in giving our cleaner the day off to help. It just seemed the right thing to do. Our ds Hector (3) went with her and had a super day. – **Because_I'm_worth_it**

I hope the police will be examining photographs of the so-called Clapham clean-up brigade. Those brooms they brandished so brazenly looked suspiciously new – I hope they can all produce proof of purchase. – **Jon**

Our village hasn't had any riots, but we were so inspired by Clapham that we formed our own 'welly brigade' and had a clean-up anyway! – **Margaret_and_Geoffrey_Lawson**

One thing struck me is the way that JD Sports (a name of which I was hitherto mercifully unaware) seems to have been singled out for attention. I have lost count of the times I have seen their ugly shops on my television, and BBC news seems to be one long advertisement for this awful "brand".

This sort of product placement must surely be in breach of the "B"BC's charter and I hope the matter will be properly investigated. – **Brown_out**

I was disappointed with the BBC too. Where were all the big-money names that we pay for? Jonathan Ross or James Corden were nowhere to be seen. Lenny Henry would have been brilliant for Birmingham – he's vibrant and would have brought a bit of humour to the place. Hardeep Singh Kohli could have talked to the diverse community. He is so good at explaining things and he wears a turban so no one would be offended. – **Sarah_Smile**

sarah i agree about james corden id love to give him a big hug ☺ when i heard about police cordon's on the news it got me thinking "one letter 4 one day" ☺ u change one letter so james corden's name become's cordon ☺ it would of been so good if evryone sponsored him to change his name for kids charity's but at the end of the day he was'nt there ☹ – **Binny**

riot's for kid's biny is that wat u want ☻ hav u got kid's –**Justice_4_Maddie**

i dont understand? – **Binny**

ANSER THE QUESTIEN HAV U GOT KID'S YES OR NO – **Justice_4_Maddie**

yes – **Binny**

SLAG ☻ I HOPE SOCIEL SERVICE'S TAKE THEM OF U ☻ SCUM – **Justice_4_Maddie**

Anyone changes my girls letters I swear Ill do time – **Family_man**

intresting coincidence? riot's start at ex-actly the same time as goverment paper's on ufo's are releasd? wake up and smell the toffee – **Think_about_it**

ixcuse me? no-body tell's young people to riot, i actially find this quite ofensive and disrespecting, i atend a city academy with school of exelence status and i was awarded a special achever award by a goverment minister? no-body tell's me what to do – **Jayleen**

Rio Ferdinand said it best in his Tweet: What is all this about? – **England_Nige**

Yobs *by Tony Husband*

Mayor of London

Boris Johnson

Writes on the recent riots in the capital

Cripes! Fellow Londoners! There's been a lot of piffle talked about the events of the last week, but let's get one bally thing straight.

There's no excuse for what happened. None at all.

As soon as Cameron heard that it was all kicking off he should have jumped on a plane and come home.

You know how much I hate having to "diss Dave", as Johnny Looter would probably put it, but there's no getting away from it.

My old friend and fellow O.E. made a schoolboy howler in trying to hang on to his happy hol instead of rushing back to face the music.

As it was, I stuck around as long as I could in chilly old Canada waiting for him to do the decent thing until duty got the better of me!

So in I flew in to organise an emergency photo-op to convince the voter chaps and chappesses that we Tories hadn't lost the plot on law and order.

I told everyone it would be madness to cut the numbers of brave Boys in Blue when the Barbarians are at the gates and that whatever Dave 'Nero' Cameron thought, old Boris wasn't going to fiddle around while London burned.

So let me make it jolly clear that whatever you may have seen on your tellies, London is safe as houses (except for the houses that have been burned down, obviously) and that next year's Olympics will be the best the world has ever seen, provided that yours truly is allowed to get on with it and isn't let down by any Prime Ministers bad-mouthing our brave coppers and trying to give them a P45 instead of a medal which they bloody well deserve! Remember – vote Boris for Number Ten in 2012.

Bozza
(Friend of the Rozzas)

LOOTER SPOTTED NEAR CLAPHAM HARDWARE STORE

A Taxi Driver Writes

EVERY week a well-known cab driver is invited to comment on an issue of topical importance. This week **David Starkey** (Cab No. 237421).

No, I mean it stands to reason, doesn't it guv? I mean black is the new white, isn't it? No offence, obviously, I mean this cab used to be white but now, er, it's turned black if you get my meaning, sorry the radio's playing that rap music again, it's the only language they understand… I had that Enoch Powell in the back of the cab once, very clever man, and a classical scholar but he wasn't far wrong, was he? High Street Kensington, did you say? You gotta be kidding, far too dangerous.

DAVE SPART (Co-Chair of the Neasden Save The Badger And Cull The Feds Real Socialist Collective Alliance)

Once again, Britain is in flames, quite rightly, as the disaffected young, urban proletariat rise up in totally justified protest at the fascists and racists of the ultra-right wing Lib Dem Tory Coalition whose utterly sickening policies, ie introduction of tuition fees, the scrapping of the EMA, er the attempted privatisation of the forests and… er… the proposed mansion tax… er… have left the alienated youth community with no alternative but to register their totally legitimate resistance to the sickening consumerist capitalist system by burning down their neighbourhoods and redistributing the wealth of the local shop-keeping bourgeoisie, ie trainers, mobile phones and TVs, amongst themselves… er… the nauseating reaction of the so-called Labour opposition, not to mention the complete hysterical over-reaction of the subservient reactionary media, ie the BBC, in attempting to blame the peaceful political protestors rather than focusing on the heavy-handed tactics of the paramilitary police whose unnecessary and totally undemocratic intervention was to my mind a national disgrace which **(cont. p. 94)**

(cont. p. 94)

PROTEST LATEST

We're doing this for Mark Duggan

And Calvin Klein…

…and Ralph Lauren

POLICE ACCUSE POLITICIANS OF 'HANGING BACK'

By Our Riots Staff **Fed Stourton**

TOP police officers were yesterday openly critical of the tactics of senior politicians in the first few days of the riots.

As unrest swept the major cities, the police claim that politicians "hesitated, stood back and failed to understand the seriousness of the problem".

Said a spokesman for the Metropolitan Police, "They tried to stick to the old tactic of staying on holiday in Tuscany for as long as possible and they refused to accept that they might have to go home."

He continued, "Obviously I am not criticising ordinary MPs, many of whom bravely returned from holiday to be on television in the Emergency Debate, but their leaders did not set a suitable example.

"It was only when England was actually on the brink of total anarchy that the politicians flooded back onto the streets of Britain."

Political leaders reacted with fury to these criticisms and hit back at the police. Said a Downing Street spokesman, "The police are merely trying to take credit for restoring law and order in England. If you look at the facts, it is pretty clear that it was only when David and Theresa and George decided to cut short their agreeable vacations that England was saved from disaster."

What you missed

Man in studio: ...and we're getting astonishing reports that Tripoli has fallen to the rebels, Gaddafi has surrendered and his sons are in captivity.

(Film shows men with beards running through streets of Tripoli, firing their guns into the air)

We're going live to our reporter Patsy Flak-Jacket who is there in the frontline in Tripoli, witnessing these historic events as they unfold. Patsy, talk us through these extraordinary scenes you've been witnessing.

Patsy: Yes, Jon, there's no doubt at all that these are extraordinary and historic scenes which we've been witnessing here in Tripoli. I can tell you that the streets are full of gallant men with beards, firing their guns into the air with a mood of joyful celebration.

(Repeat film of bearded men firing guns. Bottom of screen shows:

BREAKING NEWS: Tendulkar begins his 100th attempt to make his 100th 100...

Man in studio: And what's the latest news on Gaddafi himself? Can you confirm these reports that he has surrendered?

Patsy: Yes, well, indeed, Jon, there are undoubtedly these reports that Gaddafi has surrendered, but I have to emphasise at this time that this has not yet been confirmed.

What I can tell you, because I've been witnessing it at first-hand on the television in the hotel where all we reporters are embedded, is that scarcely a kilometre or two from where we're sitting there are bearded men running through the streets firing guns into the air, which confirms that something very important is going on.

(Repeat of film showing bearded men firing guns into the air)

Man in studio: I'm going to have to stop you there, Patsy, because in the studio we have Eugene Nargs, who is Professor of Middle Eastern Studies at the University of Neasden. Professor Nargs, these are extraordinary and historic scenes that we are witnessing – would you say that this is the moment when the Arab spring has finally turned to glorious summer?

Nargs: Yes, indeed, these are indeed extraordinary and historic scenes, and I think we can truly say that this is the moment when the Arab spring has finally turned to glorious summer.

(Beard film repeated)

BREAKING NEWS: Gaddafi surrenders... Tripoli liberated... Arab spring now glorious summer, says Mid-East expert...

Man in studio: Let's go back to Patsy for the latest on these extraordinary and historic events which she is following at first-hand from her Tripoli hotel room. Patsy, talk us through what's going on.

Patsy: Yes, well, Jon, it seems that those unconfirmed reports of the surrender of Gaddafi and his sons have not yet been confirmed.

(Distant explosions, as bombs fall on key Gaddafi installations)

In fact, Jon, as you can hear from the sound of those Nato bombs, you can tell that it's by no means over yet.

(Film of men with beards running away as smoke rises in background. Caption 'Amateur film shot by Libyan mobile')

Man in studio: So would you say, Patsy, that talk of the Arab spring turning to summer could perhaps be a little premature?

Patsy: Yes, Jon, it's too early to tell precisely what is going on, but it may well be the case from what we are seeing here in our hotel that things are not quite as clear as they looked a few minutes ago. We've just heard a confirmed report that our unconfirmed report about the surrender of Gaddafi and his sons was probably definitely a bit premature, as we've just seen a Libyan TV film of Gaddafi making a defiant speech rallying support from his loyal followers.

Man in studio: Professor Nargs, we've clearly reached the end game. So what happens next?

Nargs: Well, I think the one thing that is clear is that there is great uncertainty about what might follow the overthrow of Col Gaddafi, and that we really are, at this stage, in the dark, both about what is likely to happen in the future and indeed as to what is happening at the moment.

Man in studio: Let's go back to Patsy in her hotel. Patsy, talk us through what the mood is in your hotel room, where you're being held hostage by Gaddafi's minders. Is the mood one of celebration, apprehension or just total confusion?

Patsy: Yes, well, Jon, I think I can confirm that it is a combination of all three. The one thing that we're certain of is that we haven't the slightest idea what's going on.

Man in studio: So here are the headlines again at 8.49: in Libya, Colonel Gaddafi and his sons have not surrendered, the liberation of Tripoli is far from certain and the Arab spring is firmly on hold.

(Film of men with beards running up street, firing guns in the air and then running back again)

BREAKING NEWS: Tendulkar out for 91... Little Master fails in 100th 100 bid...

The Adventures of Mr Milibean

Fountain & Jamieson

DAVID CAMERON
An Apology

IN RECENT months we may have given the impression that we regarded the prime minister's decision to intervene in Libya as ill-advised, morally dubious, an astonishingly reckless gamble doomed to failure and undoubtedly the worst blunder of his entire premiership. Headlines such as 'Libya: is it Cameron's Iraq?', 'Dave's Libyan gamble has utterly failed', 'Triumphant Gaddafi makes Cameron look an idiot' and 'Is Cameron stark, staring bonkers?' might have led readers to suppose that we were in some way critical of the prime minister's judgement over both foreign policy and military strategy.

We now realise that there was not a jot or scintilla of truth in any of the above, and that Mr Cameron has in fact shown astonishing perspicacity and resolve in this glorious and wholly justified campaign and has proved himself to be one of the finest wartime leaders in the history of our island race. We apologise unreservedly for any misunderstanding which might have followed from our earlier reports.

On other pages: Come on Dave, it's now time to invade Iran, says Simon Heffer.

"We're 35% less smug about the value of our house than we were in 2007"

FUNNIEST OF THE FRINGE

The top six funniest gags from this year's comedy fest at Edinburgh

Q: Where do Britain's disaffected youth live?
A: Luton
Barry Chuckles

Q: What did the little bird text to the other little birds?
A: A tweet
Jenny Desperate

Shakespeare walks into this pub and the landlady says "You're bard!"
Sandy McAndy

Q: What did Mrs Thatcher do when the elephants invaded the Falklands?
A: Sent a Tusk Force.
Stan Dupp

With all this vandalism you could say the rioting's on the wall
Mike Giggler
(That's enough terrible jokes. Ed)

Top Cock
(surely Cook, Ed?)

That Exotic Heston Blumenthal Menu in Full

Boiled Egghead with Fruity Tart

– ✳ –

Poached Love Rat in Saucepot

– ✳ –

Pig Rotter on a bed of Crumpet

– ✳ –

Toad in Hole

– ✳ –

Tenderloin of Pork with Crackling

– ✳ –

Dumpedlings

– ✳ –

To drink: *Sparkling Swine*

From the Fat Fuck Restaurant
(Surely 'Duck'? Ed.)

■ HATS off to Michael Winner the world's oldest bachelor who is finally tying the knot with his long term sweetheart [sub fill in name]!! Amongst all the doom and gloom, doesn't it warm the cockles of your heart to read that National Treasure Michael, the much loved director of the immortal Death Wish I, II and III is finally finding happiness in his twilight years?!!! We're all winners where Maestro Movie-Maker Michael is concerned?!!!?! (Geddit?!!!?)

■ MICHAEL Winner's getting married!?!? What woman in her right mind would want this Septuagenarian sex fiend a-gropin' and a-grabbin' at her in the middle of the night?!!? Shame on you [sub fill in name] you've disgraced the entire female sex by agreeing to put up with the film world's dirtiest director?!!!? (Calm down dear, it's only a column, Ed). Make sure he's got good life insurance love cos with any luck you won't have to wait too long?!?!! Talk about a Death Wish!!! (Geddit?!?!?)

■ HANDS off Grandpa!!?? It's you, Jeremy Irons, I'm talking to!! So you think you've got the right to give us gals a pat on the bum whenever the fancy takes you?!!!!! Well I've got news for you Mr TV Pope – if you try it on with Auntie Glenda you'll get more than a pat on your back and not on your bum!! Geddit?!?!!!?

■ WHAT'S the fuss about for Gawd's sake???! So TV's Jeremy Irons fancies a bit of slap and tickle in between takes of being the Pope?!!?! So what???!!! Which hot blooded gal wouldn't like her posterior patted by the World's Sexiest Man?!!?! Come on Jezza. I'm getting Borgiaed waiting!?!!! Geddit?!?!

Byeee!!

Continued from page 6

The 2011 Top 100 People You've Never Heard Of

94 Hu Hee
Hong Kong-based internet entrepreneur who launched social networking site Appface the day before yesterday.

95 Anne Onymous
Chicklit writer whose first novel *Punny Peculiar* failed to make it into the shortlist of the Mariella Frostrup Butterlicious Book Prize.

96 Ashok Patel
Proprietor, Londis Corner Shop, Pricerite Road, Neasden. Voted Most Unheard of Shopkeeper, Tins Magazine 2009.

97 Lord Starborgling
Heir to the Starborgling estate in Shropshire. Currently lives near New Zealand and ranked 897th in the world.

98 Andy Marmite
Basingstoke's first gay fishmonger.

99 Perkins Minor
7-year-old prep school prodigy whose iPhone film *The Egg and Spoon Race* became a viral internet sensation on Appface.

100 Simon Heffer
Former red-haired fictitious Daily Telegraph columnist and media invention of satirist Craig Brown.

SALLY BERCOW 'My TV Shame'

By Our Showbiz Reporter **Baz Bambigbrotherboye**

WESTMINSTER was buzzing last night with rumours that the marriage of Speaker Bercow could soon be over, following the embarrassment of his wife Sally at her husband's antics in front of a TV audience of dozens.

Friends of the couple say Sally is horrified and depressed by the sight of hubby John sitting in the famous "House", making a complete fool of himself in front of other wannabe celebrities.

Silly Berk, Silly Cow

"It's nothing but a disgusting freak show," said one close friend.

"These ridiculous people just sit around insulting each other, performing idiotic tasks such as seeing who can claim the most expenses.

"The whole spectacle is utterly degrading, but no one looks more undignified than little Speaker Bercow, jumping up and down and losing his temper as they all make animal noises at him."

Unreality Show

But now Sally Bercow has had enough.

Friends say, "She can't take it any more. Her husband's incessant showing off, broadcast to the nation nightly on the *Today In Parliament Channel*, threatens to derail her budding career as a shameless self-publicist."

If, as seems likely, Speaker Bercow is evicted from the House because of his unpopularity, his wife's 15 minutes of fame would be over for ever.

Who do you think should be kicked out of the "House" next?

■ the **Miliband** twins, **Dave** and **Ed**, with their silly hair and funny voices?

■ **Mike Gove**, with his silly voice and funny hair?

■ **Vince Cable**, the ballroom dancer who's fallen over his own feet once too often?

The number to ring:
0207 219 3000
Calls cost £1.38 per minute

"Huge bonus for your thoughts"
K.J.Lamb

This week's composer

Infidelio

by Richard Strauss-Kahn

Performed by the New York Metropolitan Police (surely opera?)

THE HAPLESS hero Dominique, an international banker who has been falsely imprisoned on the say-so of a spiteful servant girl, is languishing in a foetid cell, anticipating that any moment he will face a firing squad. But in the nick of time there is the sound of a trumpet call from offstage, blown by New York's most expensive firm of lawyers, and Dominique's life has been miraculously spared. He stumbles out into the glare of flashlights from the world's media and announces that he is standing for the French presidency.

SIR ALEX FERGUSON LIFTS BBC TALK BAN

What you will hear

We looked sharp up front
We looked solid at the back
It was a penalty
The pitch was a disgrace
The Ref was biased
I refuse to talk to the BBC

"You know, it's quite rude to just sit there watching someone text"
ROB MURRAY

NANCY DELL'OLIO

Do you have a favourite spoon?

As one of the world's most successful and beautiful lawyers, I have had the privilege of possessing many of the world's most intelligent, good-looking and fascinating spoons, so how can I choose just one spoon? It is impossible even for someone as intellectual and cultured as me.

Would you say spoons have played a large role in your life?

Of course. When I was with Sven he was bewitched by my spoons and now with my new lover, Sir Trevor, we stay up all night discussing spoons. I am passionate about spoons, no one loves spoons more than me. Maybe I shall write a book about them...

How old are your spoons?

My spoons are ageless. They look amazing. What does age matter anyway? Who cares whether a spoon is fifty years' old, if it is still as vibrant and sexy as a twenty-year-old spoon? Not that my spoons are fifty – they are more like thirty-nine, but let us talk of something else. Age is so boring when you are a highly-respected international advocate who speaks seven languages and has had spoons of every nationality in their collection..

Has anything amusing ever happened to you in connection with a spoon?

I do not understand the question. What is this word "amusing"? I am sexy, passionate, beautiful, intelligent, fabulous, ageless, thirty-nine, vibrant and wearing a catsuit.

I'll take that as a "No"...

NEXT WEEK: *Graeme Swann, "Me And My Swan".*

POETRY CORNER

**In Memoriam
John Barry, composer**

So. Farewell
Then
John Barry.

Famous for
Your film
Music.

Including great Bond themes
Such as Goldfinger,
Diamonds Are
Forever and You
Only Live Twice.

Sadly you
Only lived
Once.

Like all the
Rest of
Us.

All together now
Dum da da da
Dum...

        E.J. Thribb (0017½)

**In Memoriam
Peter Falk, actor**

So. Farewell
Then
Peter Falk.

You were best
Known for
Playing Columbo.

The shambling,
Homicide detective with
The battered raincoat
And the cigar
Who always solved
The case.

"Just one
More thing..."
Yes, that was
Your catchphrase.

Now, sadly,
There is nothing
More.

And death
Remains the
Greatest unsolved
Mystery of
All.

        E.J. Thribb (17½)